Shake, Rattle, and Roll

RHYTHM INSTRUMENTS AND MORE FOR ACTIVE LEARNING

Abigail Flesch Connors

Dedication

Dedicated to the memory of my father, Rudolf Flesch, whose lifelong curiosity and creativity continue to inspire me every day.

Bulk Purchase

Gryphon House books are available for special premiums and sales promotions as well as for fund-raising use. Special editions or book excerpts also can be created to specifications. For details, contact the director of marketing at Gryphon House.

Disclaimer

Gryphon House, Inc., cannot be held responsible for damage, mishap, or injury incurred during the use of or because of activities in this book. Appropriate and reasonable caution and adult supervision of children involved in activities and corresponding to the age and capability of each child involved are recommended at all times. Do not leave children unattended at any time. Observe safety and caution at all times.

Shake, Rattle, and Roll

Rhythm Instruments and More for Active Learning

Gryphon House, Inc.
Lewisville, NC

ABIGAIL FLESCH CONNORS, MEd

Photography: Shutterstock.com

Library of Congress Cataloging-in-Publication Data

Connors, Abigail Flesch, 1957-

    Shake, rattle, and roll : rhythm instruments and more for active learning / by Abigail Flesch Connors.

        pages cm

    ISBN 978-0-87659-349-3

 1. Rhythm-Study and teaching (Preschool) 2. Education, Preschool–Activity programs. 3. Music in education. !. Title.

    GV463.C663 2015

    372.87-dc23

                              2014020244

Table of Contents

Activities Using Bells 49

Activities Using Sand Blocks 65

Activities Using Tambourines 77

Introduction

*I would teach children music, physics,
and philosophy, but most importantly music;
for the patterns in music and all the arts
are the keys to learning.*

■ **PLATO**

You were not expecting to start with Greek philosophy, were you? Yet it is fitting; Plato knew what he was talking about. If there were such a thing as early learning in a box, it would be music. Music is math, because its rhythms, beats, melodies, and harmonies are all built from fractions, ratios, and proportions. Music is oral language and early literacy, because we sing songs with meaningful words structured in beginnings, middles, and endings, just like sentences and stories. Music is science, because to explore music is to explore sound, acoustics, physical properties of materials, force, velocity, volume, and mass. Music is culture and community, as we share traditional tunes and the joy of making music together. Music is about learning itself, constructing knowledge and being drawn by that knowledge into new paths of discovery and awareness. Music is the wonder of inventing, imagining, and creating—and expressing our unique selves.

*Children must have the opportunity to participate in
active music making. To listen to music without
the opportunity to engage actively in music production
is like hearing the language without the
opportunity to communicate with anyone else.*

■ **CYNTHIA ENSIGN BANEY,**
"Wired for Sound: The Essential Connection between Music and Development"

"Criss-cross applesauce." "Fold your legs like a pretzel." "Hold a bubble in your mouth." If you are like most early childhood teachers, you have various tricks and techniques like these to get your class to settle down and be quiet. Do you ever wonder why we need these little tricks? It is because sitting down and being quiet is not a natural or comfortable state for young children. Young children are movers. They are runners and talkers and climbers and builders and jumpers and dancers and pretenders. They are not very good at sitting still, but they are excellent at playing.

Albert Einstein once said, "Play is the highest form of research." When young children play, they have no agenda except a burning need to learn and grow. They learn about themselves, their bodies, their environment, the people around them, and the larger culture they live in. Realizing that play is how children learn has two implications for what we do in the classroom. First, play is an active process that involves children's minds and bodies. Second, play is child centered and child led. Of course, this approach is not always practical or even possible, but we can and should give children opportunities to initiate and lead activities whenever we can. Most of the activities in this book are designed with this in mind.

In my music enrichment classes, whenever I announce that it is time to play instruments, the group erupts into an anticipatory chorus of *yays*, applause, and bouncing up and down. It took me a long time to figure out why young children respond so enthusiastically to the instruments. But after twenty years or so, I have a couple of hunches. Rhythm instruments are toys—at least in the eyes of young children. And they are the best kind of toys: completely open ended. There is no one right way to play a rhythm instrument; children will find a virtually infinite number of ways to play each one. This excites children's curiosity and promotes problem solving—it is like a puzzle to think of new ways to make music with each instrument. Children are curious not only about the instruments themselves, but also about what they can do with the instruments. Young children love to pretend with instruments. Where you and I see a tambourine, they see a hat, a bowl to eat from, a steering wheel, a cake, a planet, and countless other things. Some teachers may see this instinctive pretending as a distraction from learning about music, but I have long been convinced that it is absolutely vital to acknowledge and respect children's imaginations. Encouraging invention and creativity is an important charge for early childhood professionals. Most of the rhythm instrument activities you will find in this book allow for lots of active pretend play.

Moving to music is another uniquely effective way to inspire young children's curiosity and creativity. As they move, they investigate the capabilities of their growing bodies. "How high can I stretch?" "How many ways can I move my wrists, my knees, my fingers?" "What shapes can I make with my arms?" They are curious about movement concepts, which they can explore freely through moving to different styles of music. Take the concepts of *heavy* and *light*. Children can learn about them through our words. They can understand more when they pick up heavy and light objects. And when they actually move like light snowflakes or heavy elephants, that understanding becomes solidly fixed in their muscle memory. Children are curious about exploring the space around them and how they can move through it.

Music brings out expressive, imaginative movements as young children are challenged to portray the sounds they hear and the emotions they feel. This is one reason I love to use recordings of classical music and music from cultures around the world when leading movement improvisation activities. Unfamiliar music requires thought and careful listening and inspires amazing, wholly new, and inventive movement.

Children are such curious creatures.
They explore, question, and wonder, and by doing so, learn.
From the moment of birth, likely even before, humans are drawn to new
things. When we are curious about something new, we want to explore it.
And while exploring, we discover.

■ **DR. BRUCE D. PERRY,**
"Curiosity: The Fuel of Development"

How important is curiosity? Research has shown it to be a direct predictor of academic achievement. This is not surprising, yet many educational practices actually discourage curiosity. Recent studies indicate that direct instruction, or showing young children how to do something, results in children being less curious and less likely to discover new information. In other words, if I bring out an instrument and show children how to play it, they will generally follow my directions and play it the same way. However, think what will happen if I bring out the same instrument and act as a fellow learner, saying, "Hmm. Let's see what I can do with this. If I bang it on the floor, do you think it will be loud? Let's see. I wonder what it will sound like if I scratch it with my fingers. I'll try it." Then children have a very different reaction. When they take turns exploring the instrument, they will try all kinds of ways to handle it, hit it, roll it, and shake it. And almost always, I will learn new ways to create sound with the instrument that I had never thought of before.

When I first started teaching music to young children, I found their curiosity very annoying. There I would be, trying to introduce an activity using jingle bells, and all of a sudden a child would call out, "Hey, what is that inside the bells?" Other children would say, "I think it's rocks."

"No, it's not! It's little beads!" "It's bowling balls!" Everyone had an opinion.

"Um, I think they're little metal balls," I'd say. "Now let's get back to our song!" But by then it was too late—I had lost them. Half the children were peering intently into the bells, arguing heatedly (and loudly). I would watch helplessly as my lovely lesson plan flew out the window. I felt like a failure.

It took a while, but finally I caught on to the fact that young children's curiosity is more than just an inconvenience to adults. Curiosity is the desire to learn. And early education is all about nurturing and inspiring that desire. When a child asks a question, we should celebrate. He wants to know something. Our job is to respond as well as we can—and lead him to ask even more questions. Playing rhythm instruments and using movement to express musical ideas encourages constant exploration and nurtures curious minds.

It is the supreme art of the teacher
to awaken joy in creative expression and knowledge.

■ **ALBERT EINSTEIN**

If curiosity is the *how* of learning, creativity is the *why*. We do not learn in order to have a head stuffed with information. We learn so that we can grow to take care of ourselves, take care of others, contribute to our communities, and help make a better world. All these things require creativity. Creativity is not just about the arts—although the arts are an important part of developing our creativity—it is also needed in medicine, law, science, engineering, business, farming, teaching, and raising families. Everything we do requires creative problem-solving skills and innovative thinking.

Young children are naturally bursting with creativity, and it is up to us to nurture it and help these creative children grow up to become creative adults. Playful, improvisational music activities like the ones in this book stretch imaginations and inspire unconventional, inventive responses. They are literally lessons in creativity.

How to Use This Book

Early childhood educators can now choose from a vast array of children's musical recordings. Many are excellent, and I use them frequently in my own classes. However, there is still a lack of resources for leading real live music experiences with young children. Many young children today believe that music is something that comes from electronic devices. It is so important for them to experience making music and inventing movements. The National Association for Music Education (NAfME, 2013) affirms that a music curriculum for young children should be based on play and "should include many opportunities to explore sound through singing, moving, listening, and playing instruments." The activities in this book provide dozens of these opportunities, and children respond with enthusiasm and ingenuity. They are empowered by the chance to contribute their own ideas to a group activity, and group cohesion and a sense of community are strengthened when children share creative ideas with each other. It is my hope that this book will be an everyday resource for early childhood professionals to inspire active musical exploration in their classrooms.

This is a book of handy, easy-to-use activities for various instruments, styles of movement, and tie-ins with seasons, holidays, and other themes. I encourage you to read the whole book through at least once, and here is the reason: You may not use every single activity right now, but you will get ideas for activities to use with stories or in the future when your students are more focused, more physically coordinated, or better able to work together as a group.

I also hope you will use these activities as a jumping-off point to create your own activities—no one knows your class as well as you do! You know what they can do together as a group right now and what might challenge them. You know what excites them, what calms them, and what intrigues them. Enjoy these activities—and invent your own ideas—and use them to bring more music, curiosity, and creativity to your classroom.

PART ONE:
Rhythm Instrument Activities

Remember when you were four months old? I mean four months after conception, back in your mother's womb? Well, I wish you could, because that was a really exciting time in your life! That was when you were first able to hear. Hearing was the first of your senses to kick in, and it was literally the beginning of your consciousness. The first thing you were aware of was the rhythm of your mother's heartbeat. That heartbeat accompanied you, supported you, and comforted you for months, right up to the moment of your birth. It is no wonder that hearing remained your dominant sense for the first years of your life.

Although it may seem hard to believe when you are trying to get a roomful of four-year-olds to listen to you, hearing is a young child's dominant sense. Sound is the straightest path to a young child's attention, and the most powerful sound is rhythmic sound. Rhythm instruments provide a physical connection to music. We can listen to music, and we can sing music. But when we play instruments, we are connected to music in a deep physical sense. Young children often find singing problematic. The song may be at a difficult pitch for them to sing along with comfortably. They may be shy or embarrassed about singing in public. The song may be too fast for them to understand all the words. But the nonverbal quality of rhythm instruments frees children to explore music more easily and naturally, using their hands and other parts of their bodies to create different sounds.

Rhythm instruments allow a wide range of expression. Young children have much richer emotional lives than they can express in words. Playing music gives them opportunities to express themselves fully and freely. Rhythm instruments encourage creative thinking. I am constantly amazed and delighted by the imaginative ways children make music with rhythm instruments. Sometimes I can almost hear them thinking, "At last! Something where I can't make a mistake, where I'm not going to be corrected or evaluated." Rhythm instruments can be played any way children want to play them. With these activities, children are truly creators of their own learning.

We know that young children love to play rhythm instruments. But are there any real educational and developmental benefits? Let me count the ways.

- **Math:** Yes, math! Playing rhythm instruments involves keeping a beat, and the beat in music is math made audible. It is a pattern that repeats over and over. It is time divided into equal parts— ratios and proportions. Four-year-olds may not understand the vocabulary of math, but they internalize math concepts when they play instruments. Research supports this, indicating that early music training leads to better understanding of mathematical concepts. When we are actively involved in making music, we energize neuronal patterns in a way similar to what occurs when we play chess or work on complex math problems. Rhythmic music activities may be our best tools for building early math skills.

- **Language and emergent literacy:** Because rhythm and music support the brain's ability to process sights and sounds, they may help develop literacy skills. Rhythm activities often involve listening for patterns and sequences; beginnings, middles, and endings; and changes in dynamics (loud and soft sounds), all skills needed for language learning. Children who engage in active music making show stronger neural activation to pitch changes in speech and have a better vocabulary and reading ability than children who do not engage in active music making. Because young children are so engaged and focused when playing rhythm instruments, this is a tremendously effective and age-appropriate way to encourage early literacy skills.

- **Social and emotional development:** Joining in rhythmic activities with a group helps young children bond with others and builds group cohesion. Music activities are so much fun that children are motivated to behave appropriately and join in. As children sing, move, and play instruments together, they practice social skills such as taking turns, respecting others' boundaries, and listening to others' ideas in a relaxed, playful setting. These skills are vital for successful socialization and academic success. Rhythmic activities also support emotional health and happiness. Some studies indicate that oxytocin (a hormone that produces a positive feeling of social bonding) is released when people sing and make rhythmic music together. The joy of expressing oneself in music supports every aspect of learning and makes every day more meaningful and fun.

- **Science:** Young children do not want to just listen to music. They want to know how music is made, where it comes from, and why things sound the way they do. Children are so relentlessly curious. I sometimes think if adults still had that kind of curiosity, we would all be geniuses! Through rhythm instrument activities, children learn many science concepts:
  - Sounds can be loud or soft.
  - Different instruments and materials make different sounds.
  - The force with which we touch an instrument affects its sound.
  - Small instruments make higher-pitched sounds than larger instruments.
  - Sound travels through air and objects.
  - Different performance techniques, such as tapping, shaking, plucking, strumming, and scraping, create different sounds.
  - Exploring music is actually exploring and experimenting with sound, and young children are fascinated by the variety of sounds they can create.

- **Listening skills:** Rhythmic sound is a powerful tool for focusing children's attention and engaging them in an activity. It gets the whole class engaged as a group in hearing and participating in a music activity together. Rhythm instrument activities encourage active listening in which children are challenged to concentrate and focus. The skill of active listening helps children to be successful in every area of learning.

- **Physical development:** Playing rhythm instruments involves a set of physical abilities and skills. Young children's fine-motor skills are reinforced as they tap rhythm sticks together, hold sand blocks by the small knobs and scrape them, and perform other basic techniques. Abilities such as balancing bell bracelets on your head or holding a drum tucked in your elbow while tapping it with the other hand are more challenging and stretch children's skills.

- **Musical concepts:** I believe in teaching young children musical concepts in a developmentally appropriate way. They do not need to know about intervals and scales, for instance, but it is appropriate to help them learn the concepts of high sounds and low sounds. They do not need to know musical terminology to understand fast and slow. I do not talk about timbre (sound quality), but we explore the difference in the sounds made by metal instruments and wooden instruments. These kinds of explorations are more meaningful and engaging for young children than formal instruction.

Rhythm instrument activities not only inspire children's curiosity and creativity, but they also help them learn everything from math and science to literacy and social skills. Every child deserves the joy of creating music—and the educational benefits that go with it.

Activities Using Rhythm Sticks

There are many advantages to introducing rhythm sticks as the first rhythm instrument at the beginning of the school year, at least for children between ages three and five. Playing rhythm sticks produces a sharp, clear sound, which helps children to follow your rhythm or that of the recording they are playing along with. The sound helps them to keep a steady beat. Playing rhythm sticks is a natural extension of the motions involved in clapping and in patting thighs, both of which are instinctive ways young children respond to music.

Note: Unless specified, all rhythm-instrument activities are to be performed with the group sitting in a circle, with each child sitting with legs crossed.

Rhythm sticks need to be introduced carefully, however. As with all instruments, bring out one first, and demonstrate how to play safely. Hold rhythm sticks so that they are leaning on the floor. Emphasize that this is where the sticks always belong: on the floor. One teacher I know suggests resting your forearms on your thighs when sitting cross-legged; this will almost automatically put your arms in a good position to lean the sticks on the floor.

Demonstrate tapping one stick against the other gently, while holding the lower one leaning on the floor. Then, show children the scraping motion—scraping the smooth stick against the ridged one, which is leaning on the floor. Pass the pair of sticks around the circle and let each child try them out to show you they know the safe way to hold the rhythm sticks. Then you can bring out pairs of sticks for each child to use with an activity.

If, after one or two activities, you see that several children persist in playing sticks up near their heads or too near other children, they are clearly not developmentally ready to play rhythm sticks safely. Take a break for a month or two before you try the rhythm sticks again.

Toddlers and two-year-olds can play musical activities using one stick per child (they are not yet coordinated enough to use two sticks). They can gently tap the sticks on the floor, roll them on the floor with two hands, slide the sticks forward and back, and use a stirring motion close to the floor. Also, I recommend shorter sticks (8 inches) for very young children.

I do not mean for these suggestions to scare you away from using rhythm sticks—just the opposite! Rhythm sticks are a valuable learning tool and lots of fun. Young children, however, need safety rules and supervision to play them, just as they need rules to cut with scissors or play on playground equipment. When used safely, rhythm sticks are a wonderful way for young children to become engaged in creating music.

When I Wake Up

This activity is fairly easy, with one movement per verse. This makes it ideal for students at the beginning of the school year or whenever they are beginning to use the rhythm sticks. Emphasize the three-beat pattern at the end of each line.

1. Tap the sticks together to the beat as you sing to the tune of "A Sailor Went to Sea, Sea, Sea":

   When I wake up I tap, tap, tap.
   And all day long I tap, tap, tap.
   I go to sleep and tap, tap, tap.
   'Til I wake up and tap, tap, tap!

2. Additional verses:

   When I wake up I tap the floor...
   When I wake up I scrape, scrape, scrape...
       (scrape the sticks together)
   When I wake up I hammer, hammer, hammer...
       (hold one stick upright and "hammer" it with the other stick)

3. Ask the children to contribute their own ideas for stick motions. Tip: Ask the children to raise their hands if they have an idea so you may call on them. Otherwise you may have many voices piping up at once!

4. If you have a small group, you may want to go around the circle and have each child contribute an idea for a motion. Then, insert that child's name in the verse with that motion, for instance, "When Shawn wakes up he scrapes, scrapes, scrapes."

LEARNING BENEFITS

- Curiosity (exploring music and instruments)
- Fine-motor skills
- Improvisation and creative thinking
- Keeping a steady beat
- Kinesthetic awareness
- Patterns
- Rhythmic awareness
- Social skills (sharing ideas and respecting those of others)

And Then They Go to Sleep

This activity uses different stick movements and ends each verse with a quiet "bedtime."

LEARNING BENEFITS

- Curiosity
- Fine-motor skills
- Improvisation and creative thinking
- Listening skills
- Rhythmic awareness
- Science (use light force to lay the sticks on floor to "sleep")
- Social skills

1. Tap the sticks and sing to the tune of "Buffalo Gals," emphasizing taps on the last three beats of each of the first three lines:

   Two little sticks go tap, tap, tap,
   Tap, tap, tap, tap, tap, tap.
   Two little sticks go tap, tap, tap,
   And then they go to sleep. Sshh!
       (gently lay the sticks down)

2. Additional verses:

   Two little sticks go scrape, scrape, scrape . . .
   Two little sticks go swish, swish, swish . . . (hold the sticks on the floor and swish like windshield wipers)
   Two little sticks go drum, drum, drum . . . (tap floor)

3. Ask the children for more ideas for playing the sticks.

4. To support listening skills, after each verse the children can leave their sticks flat on the floor until you say, "Wake up!" Then, they can hold the rhythm sticks in the ready-to-play position, with the sticks leaning against the floor, until you begin the next verse.

Sticks on Toes

This rhythmic activity uses the sticks in a different way—on and around the feet!

1. Put on some instrumental music with a clear beat, such as a march. Children should be sitting in a circle with their feet out in front of them on the floor.

2. Experiment with different ways to keep the beat of the music with the rhythm sticks. Here are some suggestions to get you started:
   - Tap toes with the sticks
   - Tap opposite toes (tap right toes with left-hand sticks, left toes with right-hand sticks)
   - Tap the floor (left-hand sticks next to left leg, right-hand sticks next to right leg)
   - Tap toes, alternating left and right
   - Tap the floor, alternating left and right side
   - Roll the sticks on legs, out and in, to the beat
   - Pound ("jump") the sticks on the floor
   - Pound ("jump") the sticks, alternating left and right side
   - Glide the sticks (holding tops) on the floor
   - Glide the sticks on the floor, alternating left and right side
   - Tap sides of feet

   Safety note: Show the children how to hold the tops of the sticks in their fists when you make the sticks jump.

3. Ask the children for more ideas to keep the beat with the sticks.

LEARNING BENEFITS
- Curiosity
- Directionality
- Fine-motor skills
- Improvisation and creative thinking
- Keeping a steady beat
- Kinesthetic awareness
- Social skills

Quiet as a Mouse

Preschoolers love to be loud, but being quiet can be fun, too (especially for the teachers). Actually, it is a challenge to keep a quiet tone throughout this activity, with the rhythm sticks and the voice.

LEARNING BENEFITS

- Cognitive development (*soft* and *loud*)
- Curiosity
- Improvisation and creative thinking
- Phonemic awareness (rhyme)
- Rhythmic awareness
- Science (using light force to make quiet sounds)
- Social skills

1. While tapping the sticks together, chant or sing very softly to the tune of "Hot Cross Buns":
   Quiet as a mouse,
   Quiet as a mouse,
   In his little mouse house. (tap the sticks together very softly)
   Quiet as a mouse

2. Repeat the chant while quietly scraping the sticks, hammering, drumming on the floor, and any other movements the children come up with.

3. **Variation:** For fun, you can also try chanting, "Loud as a dinosaur in his big dinosaur house," but beware! No dinosaur was ever louder than a room full of preschoolers!

Simon Says, "Tap!"

In this version of Simon Says, children can have fun with all the different ways they can play the rhythm sticks while practicing their listening skills.

1. You can play the traditional way (by occasionally leaving out the words *Simon says* to signal that the children should not follow the directions), or you can make it easier by always saying, "Simon says," and letting the children focus on the directions.

2. Some ideas: Simon Says . . .
   - tap your sticks together
   - scrape your sticks
   - tap your sticks on the floor
   - tap your left stick on the floor
   - tap your right stick on the floor
   - hammer your sticks
   - roll your sticks
   - click your sticks (hold vertically and click sides together)
   - tap the ends of your sticks together
   - tap your shoes
   - tap your knees (gently)

LEARNING BENEFITS
- Curiosity
- Directionality (*left* and *right*)
- Fine-motor skills
- Kinesthetic awareness (feeling the sticks as they use them)
- Listening skills

Merrily We Roll Along

This song is a natural for rhythm sticks, which are very easy to roll on the floor with one or both hands.

LEARNING BENEFITS

- Curiosity
- Fine-motor skills
- Improvisation and creative thinking
- Keeping a steady beat
- Social skills
- Vocabulary (*merrily*)

1. Roll the sticks on the floor and sing:

   Merrily we roll along,
   Roll along, roll along.
   Merrily we roll along,
   Over the deep blue sea.

2. Additional verses:

   Merrily we tap along...
   Merrily we scrape along...
   Merrily we hammer along...
   Merrily we click along... (holding the sticks flat on the floor, click ends together)
   Merrily we slide along....(vacuuming motion)

3. Ask the children for other motions they can make with the sticks.

All the Little Sticks

Even toddlers can enjoy this activity. However, I do recommend that toddlers and two-year-olds use one stick rather than two. You will find that many children like to sing along to this one—they like the tappy-tappy-tap sequence.

1. Tap the sticks together (or on the floor if using one stick), and sing to the tune of "Glory, Glory, Hallelujah" (also the tune of "Little Peter Rabbit"):
   All the little sticks are going tappy-tappy-tap,
   All the little sticks are going tappy-tappy-tap,
   All the little sticks are going tappy-tappy-tap,
   That's what they like to do!

2. Additional verses:
   All the little sticks are going rolly-rolly-roll... (roll the sticks together on the floor)
   All the little sticks are going slidey-slidey-slide... (slide the sticks on the floor in a vacuuming motion)
   All the little sticks are going wiggly-wiggly-wiggle... (hold the sticks leaning on the floor and wiggle them)

3. Ask the children to contribute their own ideas for additional stick motions.

LEARNING BENEFITS

- Curiosity
- Fine-motor skills
- Improvisation and creative thinking
- Rhythmic awareness
- Sequence (making a sequence out of movement words)
- Social skills

Oh My Darling, Valentine

Here's a silly, fun activity for Valentine's Day or any day.

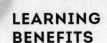

LEARNING BENEFITS

- Curiosity
- Fine-motor skills
- Improvisation and creative thinking
- Patterns (three phrases of "Oh my darling," followed by "valentine"–an AAAB pattern)
- Social skills
- Vocabulary (*valentine*)

1. Tap the sticks and sing to the tune of "Oh My Darling, Clementine":

   Oh my darling,
   Oh my darling,
   Oh my darling, valentine,
   It's so nice to tap together.
   Oh my darling, valentine.

2. Additional verses:

   It's so nice to scrape together… (scrape the sticks)
   It's so nice to hammer together… (hammer the sticks)
   It's so nice to slide together… (vacuuming motion)
   It's so nice to draw together… (hold one stick and "draw" on the floor as if it is a pencil or crayon)

3. Ask the children for more suggestions for how to play the sticks.

Tapping Softly

Use this activity to focus a group or create a quieter mood after a more boisterous activity.

1. Tap the sticks gently and softly while singing softly to the tune of "Frère Jacques":

   Tapping softly, tapping softly,
   Tap, tap, tap. Tap, tap, tap.
   Tapping softly, tapping softly,
   Tap, tap, tap. Tap, tap, tap.

2. Additional verses:

   Scraping softly...
   Scrape, scrape, scrape... (scrape the sticks together gently)
   Rolling softly... (roll the sticks on the floor)
   Jumping softly... (hold the sticks, covering the tops of the sticks with closed fists, and make the sticks "jump" gently to the beat)
   Hammering softly... (hold one stick upright to be a "nail," and hammer it gently with the other stick)
   Sliding softly... (hold the sticks by the ends and gently glide them back and forth on the floor)

3. Ask the children to contribute more suggestions for motions.

LEARNING BENEFITS

- Auditory discrimination
- Cognitive development (*soft* and *loud*)
- Curiosity
- Fine-motor skills
- Improvisation and creative thinking
- Movement vocabulary (*scraping, rolling, jumping,* and so on)
- Science (using light force to make soft sounds)
- Social skills

Free-Improvisation Ideas for Rhythm Sticks

Free-improvisation sessions with rhythm instruments are very beneficial to give children opportunities to explore the instruments and try out new ideas.

- Children can respond directly to the music with little or no verbal direction. This gives them the freedom to perform movements that cannot be easily verbalized or movements they may not perform in more structured activities.
- Improvisation provides English language learners a chance to participate more fully and easily.
- You can assess the children's listening skills. For example, are they playing in response to the music or just banging away?
- You can assess their ability to keep a steady beat.
- You can assess their level of creative thinking. For example, are they playing in familiar ways, copying their classmates, or coming up with new ideas? Remember that a style of playing, such as holding the two rhythm sticks together with one hand and tapping them on the floor, may not seem original to you but may be very new for them.

1. When you lead free-improvisation sessions, choose a rhythmic piece of music to make it easy for the children to hear the beat. If possible, use an instrumental piece—words can sometimes be distracting in this kind of activity.

2. Play along with the children yourself. Begin with familiar ways of playing, but tell the children they can play any way they want to.

3. When your class is comfortable with free improvisation and several children are showing original and creative ways of playing, you can take this one step further. Ask the children to raise their hands if they have an idea for playing that they would like to share with the group,

then encourage the group to try the child's idea. This makes the activity a more social experience, as children share their ideas with each other and respectfully listen to each other.

4. If your group seems stuck for new ideas, you can demonstrate a movement to get the children participating. For example, if you play the rhythm sticks by making them jump on the floor, children may be inspired to make the sticks march, walk, or dance. One idea leads to another. That is part of the power of improvising in a group, whether in free or structured activities—young children truly learn from and with each other. I find it helpful to write down the ideas children come up with in each session, to use again the next time we play with rhythm sticks.

Here are some suggestions to inspire new ideas:
- Swish the sticks on the floor like windshield wipers
- Hold the sticks on the floor and click the ends of the sticks together
- Hold the sticks upright and make them jump on the floor
- Pretend the sticks are skating on the floor
- Pretend the sticks are skiing on the floor
- Tap the sticks lightly on knees
- Tap the sticks on shoes
- Draw circles on the floor with the sticks
- Holding the sticks upright, sway them left and right
- Draw wiggly lines on the floor

Here are some of my favorite pieces to use for free-improvisation sessions with rhythm sticks. These songs are available via online music-purchasing websites.
- "Saturday Morning," *Everything Grows* by Raffi
- "Shortnin' Bread," *A Tisket, a Tasket, a Child's Rhythm Basket* by Brent Lewis
- "Obwisana," *Drum Like an Animal* by Tom Foote
- "Country Classics Start and Stop" (instrumental), *Rhythms on Parade* by Hap Palmer

LEARNING BENEFITS
- Curiosity
- Fine-motor skills
- Improvisation and creative thinking
- Kinesthetic awareness (feeling the sticks with hands, knees, feet)
- Science (more force needed for jumping, less for swaying and other movements)
- Social skills
- Vocabulary (*skating* and *skiing*)

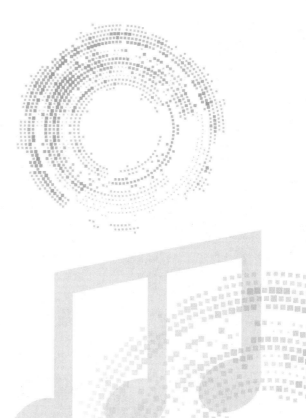

Activities Using Shakers

Hooray for shakers! Shakers, also called *maracas*, are my absolute favorite rhythm instrument for young children. Shakers are easy to play; have a wonderful, festive sound; and are incredibly versatile—they can be played in a seemingly infinite number of ways. After twenty years or so, you would think I had seen it all, but my students keep coming up with new ways to make music with shakers. For instance, recently a boy pretended his shaker was an anteater's snout and made it slide and eat ants.

The beads sliding around inside the shaker give it an imprecise and loose sound, which lends itself to fluid movements such as twirling, waving, and wiggling. Shakers are ideal for improvising to Latin American, Caribbean, and African music. The rhythms in these musical styles inspire children to think of new ways to play the shakers and new ways to move their bodies while playing.

Before beginning a shakers activity, remind the children to always put the shaker down gently when it is time to stop playing (this may require some practice). Sometimes it helps to tell the children to put the shaker down for a nap—that encourages soft and gentle handling.

The More We Shake Together

This activity helps children explore different ways to play the shakers.

LEARNING BENEFITS

- Curiosity
- Directionality (pointing out and in)
- Fine-motor skills
- Imagination
- Improvisation and creative thinking
- Patterns (this activity is in 3/4 time, or three beats per measure—a 1-2-3, 1-2-3 pattern)
- Social skills

1. Shake the shakers to the beat while singing to the tune of "The More We Get Together":

   The more we shake together,
   Together, together,
   The more we shake together,
   The happier we'll be.
   For your friends are my friends, (on *your friends* point out with shaker; on *my friends* point to self)
   And my friends are your friends.
   The more we shake together,
   The happier we'll be.

2. Additional verses:

   The more we roll together... (roll shaker on the floor like a rolling pin)
   The more we jump together... (hold "stem" of shaker and make it "jump" on the floor)
   The more we vacuum together... (glide shaker out and in on the floor like a vacuum cleaner)

3. See what other ideas the children can come up with. You may have running, flying, hopping, and dancing shakers!

Oatmeal in the Pot

Young children enjoy singing about things they are familiar with. This activity not only has the fun of everyday foods, such as oatmeal and spaghetti, it also gives children a chance to be creative by adding their own favorites or silly ideas, such as ice cream or crackers!

1. Shake the shakers in a stirring motion while singing to the tune of "If You're Happy and You Know It":

   Oh, I'm stirring up some oatmeal in the pot.
   Yum! Yum!
   Oh, I'm stirring up some oatmeal in the pot.
   Yum! Yum!
   Oh, it smells so good, just like I knew it would!
       (pretend to smell the "spoon," then nod your head)
   Oh, I'm stirring up some oatmeal in the pot!
   Yum! Yum!

2. Additional verses:

   Oh, I'm stirring up spaghetti in the pot...
   Oh, I'm stirring up some soup in the pot...
   Oh, I'm stirring macaroni in the pot...
   Oh, I'm stirring up potatoes in the pot...
   Encourage the children to insert some of their favorite foods into the song.

3. **Variation:** When the children know this song well, they can add other food-preparation motions, such as spreading jelly on bread, pouring rice in a pot, shaking salt in some soup, and so on.

LEARNING BENEFITS
- Creative thinking
- Curiosity
- Fine-motor skills
- Imagination
- Patterns (first, second, and fourth lines have the same words; third line has different words–an AABA pattern)
- Social skills

Teeny Tiny Little Shake

This activity uses different movements to play the shaker. It also helps children to discover that, just as there are small and large objects, there are also small and large movements.

LEARNING BENEFITS

- Cognitive development (*big* and *little*)
- Curiosity
- Fine-motor skills
- Improvisation and creative thinking
- Math skills (size)
- Social skills

1. Shake the shakers to the beat, and sing to the tune of "The Old Gray Mare":

   Can you do a teeny tiny little shake, (shake shaker gently in a very small motion)

   Teeny tiny little shake, (shake shaker gently)

   Teeny tiny little shake? (shake shaker gently)

   Can you do a teeny tiny little shake? (shake shaker gently)

   Now do a great big shake! (shake loudly with a large motion)

2. Additional verses:

   Can you do a teeny tiny little circle? (Make small circles in the air, and then make a large circle on the last line.)

   Can you do a teeny tiny little jump? (Hold the stem of the shaker and make it "jump" gently, about an inch above the ground. On the last line, make it jump high.)

   Can you do a teeny tiny little roll? (Roll the shaker on the ground, back and forth about 2 inches. On the last line, roll back and forth about 12 inches.)

   Can you do a teeny tiny little slide? (Hold the top of the shaker and slide it on the floor like a vacuum cleaner, about 2 inches back and forth. On the last line, slide it back and forth about 12 inches.)

3. Continue for as long as the children have ideas for new motions to try in "teeny tiny little" and "great big" versions.

My Friend Shaky

Shaky is a pretty silly name for a friend, but this whole song is pretty silly! When young children understand how the friends in this song get their names, they have a great time making up new friends with silly names!

1. Shake your shaker to the beat, and sing to the tune of "Glory, Glory, Hallelujah":

   My friend Shaky likes to shake, shake, shake.
   My friend Shaky likes to shake, shake, shake.
   My friend Shaky likes to shake, shake, shake.
   That's why I call him Shaky!

2. Additional verses:

   My friend Roly... (roll the shaker on the floor like a rolling pin)

   My friend Jumpy... (hold the shaker by the stem on the floor and make it "jump")

   My friend Stirry... (hold the shaker like a spoon and pretend to stir)

   My friend Rubby... (rub the shaker along your arm)

   My friend Tappy... (gently tap the shaker on your shoe or knee)

3. Ask the children for more silly friends. You may want to try Spinny, Swimmy, Hoppy, Walky, Kicky, Circly, and Dancy!

LEARNING BENEFITS
- Curiosity
- Fine-motor skills
- Improvisation and creative thinking
- Kinesthetic awareness (feeling the shaker on arm, knee, or foot)
- Movement vocabulary (*shake, roll, jump,* and so on)
- Phonemic awareness (adding *-y* ending to make silly names out of movements)
- Social skills

Shake to My Lou

This is a lively activity using different parts of the body.

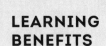

LEARNING BENEFITS

- Curiosity
- Fine-motor skills
- Improvisation and creative thinking
- Patterns (the first three lines differ from the fourth—an AAAB pattern)
- Social skills
- Spatial awareness (shaking in different places)

1. Ask the children to stand in a circle.
2. Sing to the tune of "Skip to My Lou":

   Shake, shake, shake on your knee. (rub the shaker gently and rhythmically on your knee)

   Shake, shake, shake on your knee. (rub the shaker gently and rhythmically on your knee)

   Shake, shake, shake on your knee. (rub the shaker gently and rhythmically on your knee)

   Shake to my Lou, my darling. (shake the shaker while turning around)

3. Additional verses:

   Shake, shake, shake on your shoulder... (rub the shaker gently on your shoulder)

   Shake, shake, shake on your hand... (tap the shaker gently on the open palm of your other hand)

   Shake, shake, shake on your tummy... (rub the shaker gently on your tummy)

   Shake, shake, shake on your shoe... (rub the shaker gently on your shoe)

4. **Variations:** Try shaking the shaker in different places—up high, on the floor, on your hip, on your back, on your head (gently!), and so on. With older children, challenge them to shake on less familiar parts of the body, such as their wrists, their ankles, their thighs, and so on.

The Itsy Bitsy Shaker

Like his friend the itsy bitsy spider, the itsy bitsy shaker has an adventure in the rain and the sun. He also helps children to explore different body parts.

1. Ask the children to sit on the floor.
2. Sing to the tune of "The Itsy Bitsy Spider":

   The itsy bitsy shaker walked on my arm one day.
   (hold the stem of the shaker and "walk" the shaker along your arm)

   Down came the rain, (wiggle the fingers of your other hand)

   And the shaker went away. (hide the shaker behind your back, and lay it on the floor behind you)

   Out came the sun and dried up all the rain, (make the sun's rays with your outstretched fingers)

   And the itsy bitsy shaker walked on my arm again.
   (pick up the shaker and "walk" it along your arm)

3. Additional verses:

   The itsy bitsy shaker walked on my leg one day...
   ("walk" the shaker along your leg)

   The itsy bitsy shaker walked on my head one day...
   (gently "walk" the shaker on your head)

   The itsy bitsy shaker walked on my tummy one day...
   (gently "walk" the shaker on your tummy)

4. Ask the children to suggest other body parts for the itsy bitsy shaker to walk on.

LEARNING BENEFITS

- Curiosity
- Fine-motor skills
- Improvisation and creative thinking
- Keeping a steady beat
- Kinesthetic awareness (the shaker "walks" all over the body)
- Social skills

We're Vacuuming the Floor

Children love to imitate the motions they see their parents using in household chores. This activity starts out with vacuuming the floor, but then takes a turn for the silly!

LEARNING BENEFITS

- Curiosity
- Fine-motor skills
- Imagination (pretending the shaker is a vacuum cleaner)
- Improvisation and creative thinking
- Kinesthetic awareness (feeling the shaker "vacuuming" all over the body)
- Social skills

1. Slide the shaker in a vacuuming motion on the floor while singing to the tune of "The Farmer in the Dell":

   We're vacuuming the floor.
   We're vacuuming the floor.
   Heigh-ho, the derry-o,
   We're vacuuming the floor.

2. Additional verses:

   We're vacuuming our arms... ("vacuum" along the length of your arm)
   We're vacuuming our legs... ("vacuum" along the length of your leg)

3. Ask for ideas of other body parts the children could "vacuum."

4. **Variation:** Instead of vacuuming, hold the shaker by the round part and "sweep" with the straight end on different parts of the body.

My Shaker Is a Phone

I have found that young children love to pretend that the instruments are other objects, and this activity gives free rein to their imaginations.

1. Hold the shaker to your ear, and tell the children that you are pretending it is a phone.

2. Have the children turn their shakers into phones and bounce to the beat while singing to the tune of "A-Hunting We Will Go":

   Oh, my shaker is a phone.
   My shaker is a phone.
   It's anything I want it to be.
   My shaker is a phone!

3. Additional verses:

   Oh, my shaker is a spoon... (pretend to eat with the "spoon")
   Oh, my shaker is a microphone... (sing into it)
   Oh, my shaker is a shovel... (pretend to dig with it)

4. What else could a shaker be? Your students will come up with many more suggestions!

LEARNING BENEFITS

- Curiosity
- Fine-motor skills
- Imagination (pretending the shaker is a different object)
- Improvisation and creative thinking
- Patterns (the first, second, and fourth lines have the same words; the third line is different—an AABA pattern)
- Social skills
- Vocabulary (names of different objects)

Let's Shake That Way

Whether they have been playing with shakers for a while or are trying them for the first time, all children appreciate an opportunity to explore their creativity.

LEARNING BENEFITS

- Curiosity
- Fine-motor skills
- Gross-motor skills (playing while standing or dancing)
- Improvisation and creative thinking
- Social skills

1. Explain to the children that they can play any way they wish. Give a few examples, such as, "You can play up high, on the floor, slow, fast, on your arm, on your leg, behind your back—any way you want."

2. You can ask for volunteers or go around the circle to make sure each child has a turn. The child may go to the middle of the circle when it is her turn, or you may choose to have her remain in her spot.

3. Sing to the tune of "Here We Go 'Round the Mulberry Bush":

   Let's shake the way that Jasmine shakes, (insert the name of the child who is having a turn)
   Jasmine shakes, (encourage the class to copy the child's motion with the shaker)
   Jasmine shakes.
   Let's shake the way that Jasmine shakes,
   So early in the morning.

4. Thank each child who volunteers to demonstrate a motion.

Shakety-Shakety-Shake

This activity is easy enough for all preschool-age groups.

1. Ask the children to stand in a circle while holding their shakers.

2. Gently rub your shaker on your arm, and sing to the tune of "Here We Go Looby Loo":

   Shakin' it on your arm.
   Shakin' it on your arm.
   Shakin' it on your arm.
   Shakety-shakety-shake. (shake the shaker in the air to the beat)

3. Additional verses:

   Shakin' it on your knee...
   Shakin' it on your tummy...
   Shakin' it on your head... (gently)
   Shakin' it on your shoulder...

4. Have the children suggest other body parts to shake the shaker on.

LEARNING BENEFITS

- Curiosity
- Fine-motor skills
- Improvisation and creative thinking
- Kinesthetic awareness (shaking the shaker on different parts of the body)
- Patterns (the first three lines differ from the fourth line—an AAAB pattern)
- Social skills

Going for a Walk

It might not be a good day for walking outside, but it is always a good day to go for a walk with your shaker!

LEARNING BENEFITS

- Curiosity
- Fine-motor skills
- Improvisation and creative thinking
- Movement vocabulary (*shake, jump, slide,* and so on)
- Rhythm
- Social skills
- Timbre (the difference in sound between shaking and jumping)

1. Holding your shaker upright, make it "walk" around on the floor in front of you while you sing to the tune of "Hurry, Hurry, Drive the Fire Truck":

   Going for a walk with my little shaker.
   Going for a walk with my little shaker.
   Going for a walk with my little shaker.
   Going for a walk today!

2. Additional verses:

   Going for a run...
   Going for a jump...
   Going for a spin... (hold shaker upside down on the floor and rub the handle with your hands quickly to make it spin)

3. Ask the children for more ideas.

Up and Down

This easy activity helps children explore directionality in a developmentally appropriate way.

1. Sing to the tune of "London Bridge Is Falling Down":
    Shake your shaker up and down, (slowly shake your shaker up and down in a broad, exaggerated movement)
    Up and down,
    Up and down.
    Shake your shaker up and down,
    Up and down today!

2. Remind the children not to let the shaker bang on the floor—to make it stop before it reaches the floor.

3. Additional verses:
    Shake your shaker side to side...
    Shake your shaker out and in... (shake your shaker away from your body, then back in toward your body)
    Shake your shaker front and back... (shake your shaker in front of your body, then behind your back; take this one slowly, since it is a challenge for many children)
    Shake your shaker in a circle... (twirl your shaker in a small circle)

4. Have the children suggest other ways to play.

5. **Variation:** Use this song to reinforce shape concepts with older children. They could shake their shaker in a square, a rectangle, or a triangle. One kindergartner showed me how to shake the shaker in a trapezoid!

LEARNING BENEFITS

- Bilateral coordination (crossing the midline on *side to side*)
- Cognitive development (opposites—*up* and *down*, *front* and *back*)
- Curiosity
- Directionality (up and down, side to side, front and back)
- Improvisation and creative thinking
- Math (circle shape)
- Social skills
- Spatial awareness (moving the shaker around the body, in different shapes)

Free-Improvisation Ideas for Shakers

Please see the section on "Free-Improvisation Ideas for Rhythm Sticks" for a discussion of the benefits of free improvisation and suggestions on how to lead a session.

1. Here are some suggestions for ways to play shakers to stimulate the children's imaginations.

    - Rock the shaker like a baby
    - Pretend the shaker is an elephant's trunk, and sway it from your nose
    - Sing into the shaker as if it were a microphone
    - Brush your hair with the shaker
    - Hold the shaker upside down by the large part, and shake it
    - Hold the shaker horizontally with both hands
    - Draw circles on the floor with the shaker
    - Hold the handle with both hands and shake
    - Pretend the shaker is a tail, and wag it behind your back
    - Talk into the shaker as if it were a phone
    - Make the shaker "fly" as if it were a bird or a plane
    - Hold the shaker upright, and make it "dance" on the floor
    - Hold the shaker with one hand, and pat it with the other
    - Turn the shaker around in your hands

2. Here are some of my favorite pieces to play along to in free-improvisation sessions with shakers:

    - "Cumbamba," *Putumayo Kids Presents: Jazz Playground* by José Conde
    - "Pata Pata," *Pata Pata* by Miriam Makeba
    - "Mbube," *Putumayo Kids Presents: Animal Playground* by Ladysmith Black Mambazo
    - "Meow Hou-Hou," *Baby Loves Salsa Presents: Salsa for Kittens and Puppies*

LEARNING BENEFITS

■ Curiosity

■ Fine-motor skills

■ Imagination (pretending the shaker is a different object)

■ Improvisation and creative thinking

■ Kinesthetic awareness (holding the shaker in different ways, turning it)

■ Social skills

■ Spatial awareness (holding the shaker horizontally and vertically, holding it behind the back)

Activities Using Bells

Bells introduce a whole new musical sound to young children: playing instruments made of metal, which have a distinctive sound. The sound is quite different from that made by wooden rhythm sticks or wooden or plastic shakers. The differences present great opportunities to talk about physical properties of materials in a developmentally appropriate way. Ask the children what they think the bells are made of. What else is made of metal? Their answers might include items such as cars, pots and pans, and silverware. Bring in two metal spoons and two wooden spoons. Let the children tap each pair together. Talk about how they sound different. I have heard children say that the metal spoons sound louder, harder, and "clangier." Comparing the sounds gets them thinking about how things made of different materials make different sounds when struck together.

Two varieties of bell bracelets are widely available. One kind has a hook-and-loop fastener, and another kind is sewn together. Each kind has its pros and cons. The hook-and-loop style can be taken apart, so the bracelets are more versatile. They can be held out in a straight line or attached around children's wrists or ankles for interesting music and movement activities. However, very young children often find the hook-and-loop fasteners a little too fascinating. These children may be very distracted by their ability to open the bracelets (and usually have trouble closing them again). For this reason, I recommend using the sewn-together bell bracelets when working with very young children.

Be sure to remind children that metal is hard, so we need to play the bells gently. You might want to demonstrate a light, gentle shaking motion with a bell bracelet before you hand the instruments out.

Jingle on Your Knees

Young children love a freeze dance—this variation uses bells.

LEARNING BENEFITS

- Curiosity
- Improvisation and creative thinking
- Kinesthetic awareness (feeling bells on different parts of the body)
- Listening skills (stopping on the word *freeze*)
- Patterns (jingling on one body part, then knees—an AB pattern)
- Social skills
- Vocabulary (*jingle*)

1. Jingle the bells on body parts as the song indicates, and freeze suddenly at the end of each verse. Sing to the tune of "Hush Little Baby," but sing a bit faster:

   Jingle on your arm,
   And jingle on your knees.
   Jingle on your arm,
   And jingle on your knees.
   Jingle on your arm,
   And jingle on your knees.
   Jingle your bells, and then we'll freeze! (freeze)

2. Additional verses:

   Jingle on your shoulder, and jingle on your knees...
   Jingle on your hand, and jingle on your knees... (jingle bells on the palm of your hand)
   Jingle on your tummy, and jingle on your knees...

3. Ask the children for suggestions for other body parts where you could jingle your bells.

4. **Variation:** Encourage the children to freeze their bodies in a funny shape or position when they come to the end of each verse.

Let's Jog and Jingle

This is an energetic activity that can help the children let off some steam and get the wiggles out.

1. Ask the children to stand in a circle.
2. Jog in place, and jingle your bells while singing to the tune of "Go 'Round and 'Round the Village":
    Let's jog and jingle, jingle,
    Let's jog and jingle, jingle,
    Let's jog and jingle, jingle,
    As we have done before.
3. Additional verses:
    Let's jump and jingle, jingle...
    Let's kick and jingle, jingle...
    Let's hop and jingle, jingle... (hop on one foot)
    Let's twist and jingle, jingle... (twist torso right and left)
    Let's reach and jingle, jingle... (reach alternating hands up toward the ceiling)
    Let's march and jingle, jingle...
    Let's tiptoe and jingle, jingle...
    Let's stomp and jingle, jingle...
4. Ask the children for new suggestions. Keep playing until the children are ready to stop!

LEARNING BENEFITS

- Curiosity
- Gross-motor skills (jogging in place, kicking, hopping, and so on)
- Improvisation and creative thinking
- Movement vocabulary (*jog, kick, hop,* and so on)
- Patterns (the first three lines differ from the fourth—an AAAB pattern)
- Science (light force for tiptoeing, heavy force for stomping)
- Social skills

Jingle, Jingle, Everybody

This activity is a bit tricky because it involves remembering a sequence of different parts of the body. For children under age four, you might want to sing each verse separately without going back over the other body parts. Either way, you will have lots of silly fun!

1. Jingle your bells in the air and sing to the tune of "Alouette":

   Jingle, jingle,
   Jingle, everybody.
   Jingle, jingle,
   Jingle with your bells.
   Can you jingle on your shoe?
   Yes, I jingle on my shoe.
   On my shoe, on my shoe,
   Oh-oh-oh-oh

   Jingle, jingle,
   Jingle, everybody.
   Jingle, jingle,
   Jingle with your bells.
   Can you jingle on your arm?
   Yes, I jingle on my arm.
   On my arm, on my arm,
   On my shoe, on my shoe,
   Oh-oh-oh-oh

2. Each new verse repeats the previous body parts in reverse order:

   Jingle, jingle,
   Jingle, everybody.
   Jingle, jingle,
   Jingle with your bells.
   Can you jingle on your knee?
   Yes, I jingle on my knee.
   On my knee, on my knee,
   On my arm, on my arm,
   On my shoe, on my shoe,
   Oh-oh-oh-oh

   Jingle, jingle,
   Jingle, everybody.
   Jingle, jingle,
   Jingle with your bells.
   Can you jingle on your head?
   Yes, I jingle on my head.
   On my head, on my head,
   On my knee, on my knee,
   On my arm, on my arm,
   On my shoe, on my shoe,
   Oh-oh-oh-oh

3. The children may want to suggest even more body parts. See how many you can add before you start to forget them!

LEARNING BENEFITS

- Auditory memory (remembering body parts in order)
- Curiosity
- Fine-motor skills
- Improvisation and creative thinking
- Kinesthetic awareness (feeling the bells on different parts of the body)
- Sequence (verbal order of body parts)
- Social skills

Bells Are Bouncing

This activity is easy enough for toddlers, but kindergartners will enjoy it, too.

LEARNING BENEFITS

■ Curiosity

■ Fine-motor skills

■ Improvisation and creative thinking

■ Kinesthetic awareness (feeling the bells on different parts of the body)

■ Patterns (song is in 3/4 time, or three beats per measure–a 1-2-3, 1-2-3 pattern)

■ Social skills

■ Spatial awareness (making the bells fly in the air)

1. Make the bells "jump" on the floor, and sing to the tune of "Oh My Darling, Clementine":
   Bells are bouncing,
   Bells are bouncing,
   Bells are bouncing on the floor.
   Bells are bouncing,
   Bells are bouncing,
   Bells are bouncing on the floor.

2. Additional verses:
   Bells are flying... in the air...
   Bells are climbing... on my arm...
   Bells are tapping... on my hand... (tap bells gently on opposite palm)
   Bells are twirling... on my finger... (twirl bell bracelet on your index finger)

3. Ask the children for other ideas for how the bells could move.

Jingly, Jingly, Joe

Young children love nonsense words, and there are lots of them in this very silly song.

1. Shake the bells to the beat and on the body parts indicated in the song. Sing to the tune of "Hickory Dickory Dock":

   Jingly, jingly, Joe,
   I jingle on my toe.
   I jingle up,
   I jingle down.
   Jingly, jingly, Joe!

2. After the first verse, you can pause before you name the body part in each verse, to see if the children can guess what it is. Additional verses:

   Jingly, jingly, jee, I jingle on my knee...
   Jingly, jingly joulder, I jingle on my shoulder...
   Jingly, jingly, jummy, I jingle on my tummy...
   Jingly, jingly, jed, I jingle on my head... (very gently)
   Jingly, jingly, jingers, I jingle on my fingers... (gently shake the bells on fingers of opposite hand)

3. Ask the children for ideas for other body parts to jingle.

4. **Variation:** Children love to hear their names in a song. Ask the children to volunteer different ways to play the bells. Then, as you use each child's idea, sing the child's name: "Jingly, jingly, jarah, I play my bells like Sarah," and so forth. Young children always giggle at the funny way their names sound with a *J*. Of course, if the name really does start with a *J*, you will need to improvise. How about, "Zingly, zingly, zaylen, I play my bells like Jaylen"?

LEARNING BENEFITS

- Auditory discernment (listening to the *J* word and guessing the body part it rhymes with)
- Curiosity (wondering what the next body part will be)
- Fine-motor skills
- Improvisation and creative thinking
- Kinesthetic awareness (feeling the bells on different parts of the body)
- Phonemic awareness (making nonsense rhymes with body parts)
- Social skills

When Bells Are Happy

Music can be used to express all kinds of feelings. In this activity, explore how to express some feelings with the bells.

LEARNING BENEFITS

- Cognitive development (*soft* and *loud*)
- Curiosity
- Emotional development (naming emotions)
- Fine-motor skills
- Improvisation and creative thinking
- Social skills
- Spatial awareness (playing the bells behind back)
- Vocabulary (*happy, sad, mad, shy, excited,* and so on)

1. Hold the bells with both hands, and lift the sides up to make the shape of a smile.
2. Shake the bells cheerfully, and sing to the tune of "The Wheels on the Bus":

   When bells are happy
   They sound like this,
   Sound like this,
   Sound like this.
   When bells are happy
   They sound like this.
   That's how they sound!

3. Additional verses:

   When bells are sad they sound like this... (hold the bells in the shape of a frown, and play and sing sadly and slowly)
   When bells are mad they sound like this... (hold the bells in your fist and shake hard up and down)
   When bells are shy they sound like this... (hide the bells behind back, and play and sing very softly)
   When bells are excited they sound like this... (pump air with fists and sing and play fast and loudly)

4. See if the children can think of other feelings they would like to act out with the bells.

Yankee Doodle Bells

This activity could be used for a patriotic holiday, such as Memorial Day or the Fourth of July, but it is fun to play any time. Children love thinking up wild ideas for what Yankee Doodle should ride.

1. Children should be standing in a circle. Hold the bells like the reins of a horse, gallop in place, and sing:
   Yankee Doodle went to town,
   Riding on a pony,
   Stuck a feather in his hat, (put the bells on your head like a hat and pretend to stick a feather in it)
   And called it macaroni! (keep holding the bells on your head and sway from side to side)

2. But why does Yankee Doodle always have to ride a pony? Try these:
   ...Riding on an elephant...
   ...Riding in an airplane...
   ...Riding on a motorcycle...

3. Ask the children to share other silly ideas for this song.

4. **Variation:** Your class may want even more silliness (and creativity). Have one child think of a vehicle and another think of something else Yankee Doodle could call his feather. Why not *spaghetti*? Or *chicken nuggets*? Children never want to stop this activity.

LEARNING BENEFITS
- Curiosity
- Fine-motor skills
- Gross-motor skills (galloping)
- Improvisation and creative thinking
- Social skills (sharing ideas and respecting those of others)
- Vocabulary (*elephant, airplane, motorcycle*)

Jingle and Jump

Children love this lively activity. Make sure everyone has plenty of space to play without bumping into anybody.

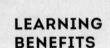

LEARNING BENEFITS

- Curiosity
- Fine-motor skills
- Gross-motor skills
- Improvisation and creative thinking
- Social skills (sharing ideas and respecting those of others)

1. Children should be standing in a circle. Sing to the tune of the "Dinah, Won't You Blow" section of "I've Been Working on the Railroad":

   Jingle and jump,
   Jingle and jump,
   Jingle, jingle, jingle, and
   Jump, jump, jump!
   Jingle and jump,
   Jingle and jump,
   Jingle, jingle, jingle, and jump! (On *jingle*, shake the bells; on *jump*, jump)

2. You can use these additional verses for variations:

   Jingle and kick...
   Jingle and wiggle... (wiggle whole body)
   Jingle and hop... (hop on one foot)
   Jingle and stomp... (stomp one foot)
   Jingle and shrug... (shrug shoulders)

3. See how many actions the children can think of to add to this song.

Jingle All Around

This activity explores the concept of opposites. With two- and three-year-olds, you may choose to just lead this activity without talking about this concept. However, older children will be ready to understand that we are using the bells to illustrate pairs of opposites.

1. Jingle the bells as indicated and sing to the tune of "Merrily We Roll Along":
   Jingle high and jingle low,
   Jingle high, jingle low,
   Jingle high and jingle low,
   And jingle all around. (make a circle in the air with the bells)

2. Additional verses:
   Jingle here and jingle there... (jingle the bells on one side of your body and then on the other side)
   Jingle soft and jingle loud...
   Jingle fast and jingle slow...

3. Ask the children if they know any more words that are opposites. You might try to portray their ideas with the bells. For instance, *day* and *night* could be shown by playing the bells energetically, then lying them down to "sleep" on the floor.

LEARNING BENEFITS

- Cognitive development (learning the concept of opposites such as *high* and *low*, *soft* and *loud*, *fast* and *slow*)
- Curiosity
- Fine-motor skills
- Improvisation and creative thinking
- Shapes (circle)
- Social skills (sharing ideas and respecting those of others)
- Vocabulary (words that are opposites)

Jingle Along with Me

One of the nice features about bells is that, unlike some other instruments, they can be played easily and safely while standing. Children move their bodies as well as their bells in this activity.

LEARNING BENEFITS

- Curiosity
- Fine-motor skills
- Gross-motor skills (stamping feet, bending knees)
- Improvisation and creative thinking
- Movement vocabulary (*stamping, bending,* and so on)
- Social skills (sharing ideas and respecting those of others)

1. Children should be standing in a circle. Jingle your bells and move as indicated while singing to the tune of "Buffalo Gals":

   Jingle your bells and stamp your foot,
   Stamp your foot, stamp your foot,
   Jingle your bells and stamp your foot,
   Jingle along with me.

2. Additional verses you can act out:

   Jingle your bells and bend your knees...
   Jingle your bells and turn around...
   Jingle your bells and nod your head...

3. Ask the children to volunteer other movement ideas for this activity.

Caterpillar

Young children like to try new movements with the rhythm instruments, and in this activity they detach the hook-and-loop fastener on the bell bracelets and lay them flat on the floor. The children tend to be curious about these fasteners, and this gives them a chance to manipulate the bracelets in a different way. Children also enjoy the fun of the caterpillar's progress in climbing.

1. Children should be holding the ends of bell bracelets that have been flattened by detaching the hook-and-loop fasteners. Gently shake the bell bracelet on the floor while singing to the tune of "The Acorn Song":

   Caterpillar, caterpillar, on the floor,
   Caterpillar, caterpillar, on the floor,
   Caterpillar, caterpillar, on the floor,
   Jingle, jingle, jingle, you're on the floor.
   Then the caterpillar starts to climb... (move as indicated)
   Caterpillar, caterpillar, on my foot...
   Caterpillar, caterpillar, on my knee...
   Caterpillar, caterpillar, on my tummy...
   Caterpillar, caterpillar, on my neck...
   Caterpillar, caterpillar, on my ear...
   Caterpillar, caterpillar, on my head...

2. Ask the children if they would like the caterpillar to climb back down. You could sing the verses in reverse order or just gently make the caterpillar crawl down and off your body.

LEARNING BENEFITS

- Curiosity
- Fine-motor skills
- Kinesthetic awareness (feeling the bells all over the body)
- Rhythmic awareness (singing the strong rhythm of "caterpillar, caterpillar, on my _____")
- Sequence (caterpillar goes up the body, then down the body, on body parts in a certain sequence)

Free-Improvisation Ideas for Bells

Please see the section on "Free-Improvisation Ideas for Rhythm Sticks" for a discussion of the benefits of free improvisation and suggestions on how to lead a session.

1. Here are some suggestions to stimulate creative thinking for playing the bells:
   - Pat hip with the bells
   - Tap the bells gently on opposite palm
   - Gently clap, with one hand holding the bells
   - Cover the bells in cupped hands and shake
   - Make the bells "fly"
   - Hold the bells with both hands and shake
   - Swing the bells side to side
   - Twirl the bells on an index finger (After trying this, one child commented, "My finger feels dizzy!")
   - Stretch your legs out and tap the bells on your toes
   - Shake the bells high over your head
   - Hold the bells with both hands and peek through the middle
   - Twirl the bells on the floor with your index finger
   - Balance the bells on your head and try to stand up and sit down

2. Here are some of my favorite pieces (available via online music-purchasing websites) to play along to in free-improvisation sessions with the bells:
   - "A Medley," *A Tisket, a Tasket, a Child's Rhythm Basket* by Brent Lewis
   - "Silver Bells That Ring in the Night," *Toot Toot!* by the Wiggles
   - "Ying Chun Flowers," *Chinese New Years Music* by the Heart of the Dragon Ensemble
   - "Sleigh Ride–German Dance No. 76," *Moving with Mozart* by Mozart from Kimbo Educational

LEARNING BENEFITS

- Balance
- Curiosity
- Crossing the midline (tapping the bells on opposite palm, swinging the bells side to side)
- Fine-motor skills
- Gross-motor skills (stretching out legs, standing, and sitting)
- Improvisation and creative thinking
- Movement vocabulary (*twirl, peek, balance*)
- Social skills (sharing ideas and respecting those of others)

Activities Using Sand Blocks

At first glance, you would not think there would be very many ways to play sand blocks. You can scrape them together to make that great "sh-sh-sh-sh" sound. You can clap them together (though probably not more than once—it is really, really loud). And that is about it, right? Well, not if you have the imagination of a young child. To young children, all instruments (and all activities, for that matter) are open to unlimited improvisation.

Aside from requesting that they avoid clapping the sand blocks together (except in certain situations), I accept any and all creative ideas children may have for playing music with sand blocks.

Often, children will tap the sand blocks together horizontally, vertically (with the blocks side to side "standing up"), end to end, or one on top of the other. They will make them jump on the floor, their shoes, and their knees. I have seen children open and close the sand blocks like a book or a door and many other creative motions.

It reminds me of something I once learned in a class on improvisational comedy. The longer you improvise, the more original and interesting your ideas become. In other words, if you improvise for two minutes, you may come up with a few relatively conventional ideas. But if you do it for ten minutes, you will find yourself mentally stretching to create fresh, imaginative ideas.

You can purchase sand blocks with or without handles on the nonsandpaper side. I like the kind with handles, which I find are easier for young children's play.

The Little Train

This activity takes advantage of the "choo-choo train" sound of scraping the sand blocks. It also has almost limitless possibilities for creativity and just plain silliness, as the children imagine what they may find on the train tracks!

1. Scrape the sand blocks and sing to the tune of "Polly Wolly Doodle":
   The little train went down the track,
   Going chugga-chugga-choo-choo all day,
   When all of a sudden, it had to stop (clap blocks once on *stop*)
   'Cause something was in its way.
   It was an elephant, it was an elephant, (on, *It was an elephant,* and through the end of the song, stomp blocks on the floor facedown, to the beat, like an elephant stomping)
   Stomping across the tracks!
   It was an elephant, it was an elephant,
   Stomping across the tracks!

2. Additional verses you can use:
   ... It was a bird, it was a bird,
   Flying across the tracks... (hold blocks like wings and make them "fly")
   ...It was a kangaroo, it was a kangaroo,
   Jumping across the tracks... (make the sand blocks "jump" on the ground)
   ...It was a duck, it was a duck,
   Waddling across the tracks...(hold the sand blocks like duck feet and make them "waddle")
   ...It was a horse, it was a horse,
   Galloping across the tracks... (make the sand blocks "gallop" on the floor)

3. Continue, with children contributing ideas for animals, vehicles, and people (airplanes? ballerinas?) to "cross the tracks."

4. **Variation:** Instead of a little train, the activity could be about a little boat. You could sing *"The little boat sailed through the sea, Going zoomy-zoomy-zoomy all day..."* and proceed with the rest of the song. This time, the children can think of things that might block the boat's path in the sea: a whale? a big wave? a shark? How can they act out these ideas with the sand blocks?

LEARNING BENEFITS

- Curiosity
- Fine-motor skills
- Improvisation and creative thinking
- Imagination (pretending the sand blocks are other objects)
- Patterns (the song is in two sections: "The little train" section and the "it was a _____" section—an AB pattern)
- Social skills (sharing ideas and respecting those of others)

Little Frogs

Pretend the sand blocks are frogs in this activity. Many picture books feature frogs, and this can be a nice tie-in activity.

1. Hold the sand blocks facedown on the floor, and make them do very small hops while you sing to the tune of "Jimmy Crack Corn":

   Little frogs, little frogs, hop like this,
   Little frogs, little frogs, hop like this,
   Little frogs, little frogs, hop like this,
   Little frogs hop like this.

2. Additional verses you can use:

   Big frogs, big frogs, hop like this... (make bigger hops)
   Little frogs, little frogs, swim like this... (move the sand blocks on the floor in a wavy, swimmy motion)
   Little frogs, little frogs, catch a fly... (hold the sand blocks and clap them in the air to "catch a fly")

3. Add more motions as the children suggest them.

LEARNING BENEFITS

- Cognitive development (concepts of *big* and *small*)
- Curiosity
- Fine-motor skills
- Imagination (pretending the sand blocks are frogs)
- Improvisation and creative thinking
- Social skills (sharing ideas and respecting those of others)

Elevator

This is a fun chanting game for older groups (four- and five-year-olds). It can be challenging because, instead of just down and up or bottom and top, it goes through steps that get a little higher each time.

1. Scrape blocks together on the floor and chant:
   Elevator, elevator,
   On the first floor,
   It shakes (jostle the sand blocks side to side a bit)
   And it bumps (clap the sand blocks on the word
        bumps)
   And it goes up some more. (keeping the sand blocks
        together, slowly bring them up a few inches)

2. Sing the second verse:
   Elevator, elevator,
   On the second floor... (same as the first verse; rise a
        few more inches at the end)

3. Continue until the fifth floor. Then, have the elevator "go down some more" at the end of each verse until it reaches the bottom again.

4. **Variation:** As an alternate ending and to make it a shorter activity, end with this verse:
   Elevator, elevator,
   Fifth floor now,
   It shakes and it bumps and goes all the way down!
        (on "all the way down," bring the sand blocks down
        to the floor)

LEARNING BENEFITS
- Counting (ordinal numbers)
- Curiosity
- Directionality (up and down)
- Fine-motor skills
- Imagination (pretending the sand blocks are an elevator)
- Rhythmic awareness (chant has a strong rhythm)

Chugging Down the Track

I took the old song "There's a Hole in the Bottom of the Sea" as a model for this activity. In the tradition of that old favorite, it makes absolutely no sense, but it is fun to sing.

1. Scrape the sand blocks together and sing to the tune of "There's a Hole in the Bottom of the Sea":

   There's a train that's chugging down the track,

   There's a train that's chugging down the track,

   There's a train, there's a train,

   There's a train that's chugging down the track.

2. Sing the second verse:

   There's a horse on the train that's chugging down the track, (holding the sand blocks facedown, make them gallop on the floor; on the word *train*, scrape them)

   There's a horse on the train that's chugging down the track,

   There's a horse, there's a horse, (gallop)

   There's a horse on the train that's chugging down the track.

3. Sing the third verse:

   There's a bird on the horse on the train that's chugging down the track, (hold the sand blocks like wings and "fly," then gallop, then scrape)

   There's a bird on the horse on the train that's chugging down the track,

   There's a bird, there's a bird, (fly)

   There's a bird on the horse on the train that's chugging down the track.

4. Sing the fourth verse:

*There's a bug on the bird on the horse on the train
that's chugging down the track,* (hold the sand
blocks facedown and have them crawl on the floor,
then fly, then gallop, then scrape)
*There's a bug on the bird on the horse on the train
that's chugging down the track,
There's a bug, there's a bug,* (crawl)
*There's a bug on the bird on the horse on the train
that's chugging down the track.*

5. You may have a group who wants to add even more
verses to the song. Maybe they would like to have a
dinosaur on the train!

LEARNING BENEFITS

- Auditory discernment
  (changing motions according
  to the words of the song)
- Auditory memory
  (remembering the objects in
  order)
- Curiosity
- Fine-motor skills
- Imagination (pretending the
  sand blocks are a train and
  other objects or animals)
- Improvisation and creative
  thinking
- Social skills (sharing ideas
  and respecting those of
  others)

If I Were a Bird

This easy activity lets children explore animals and the different ways that they move. If you have a small group, you may want to ask each child which animal he would like to be.

LEARNING BENEFITS

- Curiosity
- Fine-motor skills
- Imagination (pretending the sand blocks are animals)
- Improvisation and creative thinking
- Movement vocabulary (*swim*, *wiggle*, *stomp*, and so on)
- Patterns (the first three lines of each verse have the same words; the fourth line is different—an AAAB pattern)
- Social skills (sharing ideas and respecting those of others)

1. Hold the sand blocks in the air together like the wings of a bird, and flap them while singing to the tune of "The Wheels on the Bus":

   If I were a bird I'd fly, fly, fly,
   Fly, fly, fly, fly, fly, fly,
   If I were a bird I'd fly, fly, fly,
   All through the town.

2. Additional verses:

   If I were a frog I'd jump, jump, jump,
   Jump, jump, jump, jump, jump, jump,
   If I were a frog I'd jump, jump, jump,
   All through the town. (hold the sand blocks facedown on the floor and make them jump)

   If I were a fish I'd swim, swim, swim... (scrape the sand blocks in a swimmy motion)

   If I were a snake I'd wiggle, wiggle, wiggle... (hold the sand blocks together and wiggle them on the floor)

   If I were a dinosaur I'd stomp, stomp, stomp... (hold the sand blocks facedown and stomp heavily on the floor)

3. Other ideas might include a turtle (walk very slowly), a rabbit (hop), a monkey (climb a tree), a duck (waddle), and a bug (crawl). Have children contribute their ideas for animals.

Pease Porridge Hot

Do any of your students know what *porridge* is? It is one of those words like *tuffet* that seems to be much more common in nursery rhymes than in real life. Children are usually curious about what *pease porridge* is. It is an old-fashioned pudding made of peas.

1. Start by practicing the rhythm of tapping and clapping you will use to accompany the rhyme. (It is the same rhythm as the patting-clapping accompaniment to "We Will Rock You" at sports events.)

   Tap, tap (tap the sand blocks facedown on floor)

   Clap! (clap the sand blocks together)

2. Here's the rhyme to chant:

   Pease porridge hot!

   Pease porridge cold!

   Pease porridge in the pot

   Nine days old!

   Some like it hot,

   And some like it cold,

   And some like it in the pot

   Nine days old!

3. When you've got the rhythm down, you can have fun with mixing up some of the other musical elements. Try playing and chanting very softly, very loudly, very slowly, and very fast. Or try chanting in a high, squeaky voice; in a deep, low voice; and so on.

4. **Variation:** When the children are familiar with this activity, invite them to come up with new ways to express the rhythm pattern (AAB). For example, they could tap the sides of the blocks together twice and then tap them facedown on the floor.

LEARNING BENEFITS

- Cognitive development (concepts of *soft* and *loud, slow* and *fast*)
- Curiosity
- Fine-motor skills
- Kinesthetic awareness (feeling the difference in the throat and chest when singing in a very high voice and in a very low voice)
- Rhythm (the chant has a strong, persistent rhythm)
- Vocabulary (*pease porridge*)

All the Little Ducks

Sand blocks become the webbed feet of little ducks in this activity. This would be a good tie-in to reading a story about ducks or would work well in a unit on farm animals.

LEARNING BENEFITS

- Curiosity
- Fine-motor skills
- Imagination (pretending the sand blocks are ducks)
- Improvisation and creative thinking
- Movement vocabulary (*waddle, swim, fly*, and so on)
- Science (light force is used to gently lay ducks down to "sleep")
- Social skills (sharing ideas and respecting those of others)

1. Hold the sand blocks together, and open and close them like a quacking beak while singing to the tune of "The Wheels on the Bus":

   All the little ducks go quack, quack, quack,
   Quack, quack, quack,
   Quack, quack, quack,
   Oh, all the little ducks go quack, quack, quack,
   All around the pond.

2. Additional verses:

   All the little ducks go waddle, waddle, waddle... (hold the sand blocks facedown on the floor, and make them waddle)

   All the little ducks go swim, swim, swim... (scrape the sand blocks together on the floor in a swimming motion)

   All the little ducks go fly, fly, fly... (hold the sand blocks in the air like wings and flap them)

   All the little ducks go sleep, sleep, sleep... (gently lay the sand blocks facedown on the floor and sing quietly)

3. Discuss what else the little ducks could do. Your students will have some great ideas!

Free-Improvisation Ideas for Sand Blocks

Please see the section on "Free-Improvisation Ideas for Rhythm Sticks" for a discussion of the benefits of free improvisation and suggestions on how to lead a session.

To help inspire your students to come up with new ideas, try some interesting techniques such as these:

- Hold the sand blocks facedown in the air, and tap the sides together
- Gently make the sand blocks jump on your knees
- Stretch out your legs and gently tap the sand blocks on your toes
- Hold the sand blocks facedown on the floor, and slide them out, away from the body, and back in
- Scrape the sand blocks high in the air
- Try to scrape them behind your back
- Hold the sand blocks by the handles and twirl them
- Hold the sand blocks like an open book, and then open and shut them to the beat
- "Stomp" the sand blocks facedown, alternating left and right, like a bear
- Tap the sides while holding the sand blocks facedown on the floor
- Hold the sand blocks upright, and make them walk
- Hold the sand blocks "backwards," and tap the handles together

LEARNING BENEFITS

- Curiosity
- Fine-motor skills
- Imagination (pretending the sand blocks are books, bears, and other things)
- Improvisation and creative thinking
- Social skills (sharing ideas and respecting those of others)
- Spatial awareness (scraping the sand blocks in the air, behind your back, and so on)

Here are some of my favorite pieces (available via online music-purchasing sites) to play along to in free-improvisation sessions with sand blocks:

- "Five Little Monkeys" (instrumental version), *So Big* by Hap Palmer
- "The Mountain Polka," *Everything Grows* by Raffi
- "Over the River and Through the Woods," *Three Silly Kittens* from Kimbo Educational
- "Linus and Lucy," *A Charlie Brown Christmas* by Vincent Guaraldi

Activities Using Tambourines

Tambourines have been a part of human musical culture since ancient times. There are headless tambourines as well as those with a head, usually made of animal skin or plastic. (Children's tambourines usually have plastic heads.) I love tambourines because they combine the physical qualities of the drum with the bright jingle of metal. (Trivia fact: Did you know the jingles on tambourines are called *zils*?)

Now here is the bad news about tambourines: They are extremely loud, especially when many excited young children are banging on them with their whole hands. You know when you say, "If we're too loud, it's going to hurt our ears"? Well, the sound of many tambourines being hit hard can actually harm children's hearing. This is true of any loud sound, by the way. A good rule of thumb is that if you are comfortable talking over a sound, then it is at a low enough decibel level to be healthy. So, the number-one rule for tambourines is to tap them with one or two fingers. That is enough force to make a satisfying sound.

Here is a good way to get children in the habit of tapping the tambourine with one finger: Show them your pointer finger, and tell them it is your special tambourine-tapping finger. Ask them to hold up their tapping fingers, and practice tapping on the floor with them. Then, bring out the tambourines.

When played at a healthy sound level, tambourines are a wonderful instrument for young children to explore. The joyful sound and the musical versatility of the tambourine are fascinating for young children, and they respond enthusiastically.

I Can Tap My Tambourine

This is an easy activity for exploring some of the different ways we can make music with the tambourine.

LEARNING BENEFITS

- Curiosity
- Fine-motor skills
- Patterns (the first three lines of every verse have the same words; the fourth line is different–an AAAB pattern)
- Imagination (pretending the tambourine is a steering wheel)
- Improvisation and creative thinking
- Social skills (sharing ideas and respecting those of others)

1. Before you begin the song, remind the children to tap the tambourine with their pointer finger rather than their entire hand. This creates a more pleasant sound, especially when many children are playing together.

2. Tap the tambourine with your pointer finger while singing to the tune of "A Sailor Went to Sea" (when tapping, emphasize the three-note rhythm of "tam-bour-ine" with this song):

   Oh, I can tap my tambourine,
   Oh, I can tap my tambourine,
   Oh, I can tap my tambourine,
   We all can tap our tambourines!

3. Additional verses:

   Oh, I can shake my tambourine... (shake the tambourine gently)
   Oh, I can pat my tambourine... (softly pat the tambourine on your hip)
   Oh, I can drive my tambourine... (pretend to "drive" the tambourine like a steering wheel)
   Oh, I can roll my tambourine... (roll the tambourine on the floor)

4. Ask the children to think of more ways to play the tambourine.

Jumping on the Floor

When I started using tambourines with young children, I did not think of making the tambourines jump. Once again, the children taught me that anything can jump! Here is a song about a jumping tambourine.

1. Hold the tambourine, head facing up, in both hands (with fingers in the holes rather than under the tambourine). Gently make it jump on the floor.

2. Sing to the tune of "If You're Happy and You Know It":
   Oh, my tambourine is jumping on the floor,
   Oh, my tambourine is jumping on the floor,
   Oh, it's jumping on the floor, like it never did before,
   Oh, my tambourine is jumping on the floor!

3. Additional verses:
   Oh, my tambourine is rolling on the floor... (roll the tambourine vertically back and forth on the floor)
   Oh, my tambourine is sliding on the floor... (hold the tambourine at an angle to the floor, and slide it along the floor like a vacuum cleaner)
   Oh, my tambourine is jumping upside down... (hold the tambourine with both hands, head facing down, and gently make it jump on the floor)
   Oh, my tambourine is spinning on the floor... (hold the tambourine vertically on the floor, and use both hands to turn it and make it spin)

4. Ask the children for other ways to play the tambourine.

5. **Variation:** Use the pattern of the song "If You're Happy and You Know It." Sing without playing until the end of the first, second, and fourth lines, when you do the motion twice. For instance, "Oh, my tambourine is jumping on the floor (jump, jump)..."

LEARNING BENEFITS

- Curiosity
- Directionality (playing the tambourine upside down)
- Fine-motor skills
- Improvisation and creative thinking
- Movement vocabulary (*jumping, sliding, rolling,* and so on)
- Social skills (sharing ideas and respecting those of others)

We're Driving 'Round the Village

One of the first things many young children do with a tambourine is to drive it like a steering wheel. It is even more fun than a real steering wheel, since it makes so much jingly noise.

LEARNING BENEFITS

- Curiosity
- Fine-motor skills
- Imagination (pretending to drive the tambourine like a steering wheel)
- Improvisation and creative thinking
- Patterns (the first three lines of each verse have the same words; the fourth line is different—an AAAB pattern)
- Social skills (sharing ideas and respecting those of others)
- Vocabulary (*village, scratching*)

1. Hold the tambourine like a steering wheel, and "drive" while singing to the tune of "Go 'Round and 'Round the Village":

   We're driving 'round the village,
   We're driving 'round the village,
   We're driving 'round the village,
   As we have done before!

2. Additional verses:

   We're tapping 'round the village... (tap the tambourine)
   We're shaking 'round the village... (shake the tambourine)
   We're scratching 'round the village... (scratch the tambourine with fingernails)

3. Have the children contribute more ways to go "'round the village" with the tambourines.

Tapping My Tambourine

This is another easy activity for exploring new ways to make music with the tambourine.

1. Tap the tambourine to the beat with your pointer finger while singing to the tune of "Shoo, Fly, Don't Bother Me":

   Tapping my tambourine,
   Tapping my tambourine,
   Tapping my tambourine,
   Tap, tap, tap my tambourine.

2. Additional verses:

   Shaking my tambourine...
   Patting my tambourine... (pat the tambourine on knee or hip)
   Wearing my tambourine... (hold the tambourine on your head like a hat and bounce to the beat)

3. Ask the children to suggest other ways to play the tambourine.

LEARNING BENEFITS

- Curiosity
- Fine-motor skills (using pointer finger to tap)
- Imagination (pretending the tambourine is a hat)
- Improvisation and creative thinking
- Keeping a steady beat
- Kinesthetic awareness (feeling the tambourine patting on the knee or hip)
- Social skills (sharing ideas and respecting those of others)

Tambourines Are Falling Down

This simple activity is easy enough for toddlers yet can be used as a creative challenge for older children.

LEARNING BENEFITS

- Curiosity
- Directionality (falling-down motion)
- Fine-motor skills
- Improvisation and creative thinking
- Rhythmic awareness (most verses have a three-beat rhythm at the end of the first three lines)
- Social skills (sharing ideas and respecting those of others)

1. Hold the tambourine with both hands, and make it "fall" from up high like rain, over and over, to the beat. Sing to the tune of "London Bridge Is Falling Down":

   Tambourines are falling down,
   Falling down, falling down,
   Tambourines are falling down,
   My fair lady.

2. Additional verses:

   Tambourines go tap, tap, tap... (tap the tambourine, emphasizing the beats on "tap, tap, tap")
   Tambourines go shake, shake, shake... (shake the tambourine)
   Tambourines go pat, pat, pat... (pat the tambourine on the hip)

3. Older students can be encouraged to come up with more ways to play the tambourine.

I'm Marching and I'm Tapping

This fun activity requires a certain amount of coordination. It would be an excellent choice for four- and five-year-olds. They love trying tricky things.

1. Children should be standing in a circle holding their tambourines. March in place and lightly tap the tambourine while singing to the tune of "The Farmer in the Dell":

   I'm marching and I'm tapping,
   I'm marching and I'm tapping,
   Heigh-ho, the derry-o,
   I'm marching and I'm tapping.

2. Additional verses:

   I'm kicking and I'm tapping... (kick alternating feet while lightly tapping the tambourine)

   I'm turning and I'm tapping... (lightly tap the tambourine while turning around)

   I'm tiptoeing and I'm tapping... (tiptoe in place while lightly tapping the tambourine)

3. Challenge the children to come up with more ideas for ways to move while tapping the tambourine. Jumping or hopping is probably not a good idea. It is hard to control the tambourine while jumping. How about nodding, blinking, swaying, or stomping?

4. **Variation:** Older children could think of ways to do two different motions. Instead of marching and tapping, they could kick their feet and shake the tambourine or bend their bodies and scratch the tambourine. The possibilities are practically endless!

LEARNING BENEFITS

- Coordination (tapping the tambourine while using the feet to keep the beat in different ways)
- Curiosity
- Fine-motor skills
- Gross-motor skills (marching, kicking, turning, tiptoeing, and so on)
- Improvisation and creative thinking
- Social skills (sharing ideas and respecting those of others)

Tapping at the Window

This chant encourages careful listening and counting. It also features a sudden stop at the end of each verse, which young children always enjoy.

LEARNING BENEFITS

- Auditory memory (remembering the verbal cue without prompting)
- Curiosity
- Fine-motor skills
- Improvisation and creative thinking
- Listening skills (stopping on the cue of the word *FOUR*)
- Movement vocabulary (*scratching, knocking, pounding,* and so on)
- Social skills (sharing ideas and respecting those of others)

1. Lightly tap the tambourine with your pointer finger while you rhythmically chant:
   Tapping at the window,
   Tapping at the door,
   But we will stop at the count of four.
   (a bit more slowly) *One-two-three-FOUR!* (tap on each number and stop suddenly on *FOUR*)
2. Additional verses:
   Scratching at the window... (scratch the head of the tambourine with your fingers)
   Knocking at the window... (lightly knock on the head of the tambourine)
   Pounding at the window... (lightly pound on the head of the tambourine with your fist)
3. Children can volunteer other ways you might play "at the window."
4. **Variation:** When children know this song well, they may enjoy the challenge of stopping on other numbers. Can they stop at the count of six or nine?

Free-Improvisation Ideas for Tambourines

Please see the section on "Free-Improvisation Ideas for Rhythm Sticks" for a discussion of the benefits of free improvisation and suggestions on how to lead a session.

These different techniques can encourage children to come up with their own new and unusual ideas for ways to play the tambourine.

- Rub the head of the tambourine with the palm of your hand
- Tap the tambourine softly while holding it on your head
- Pretend your tambourine is a dish, and "eat" out of it to the beat
- Turn the tambourine upside down, and tap the inside of the head
- Tap the jingles on the outside of the tambourine
- Hold the tambourine with both hands and gently shake it
- Lightly pat the tambourine on your arm
- Very lightly tap the tambourine with your elbow
- Turn the tambourine around in your hands
- "Strum" the head of the tambourine like a guitar
- Hide your face behind the tambourine, and gently tap the head of the instrument
- Stretch your legs out, and softly pat the tambourine on your toes

LEARNING BENEFITS

- Curiosity
- Directionality (turning the tambourine upside down)
- Fine-motor skills
- Gross-motor skills (stretching legs out and patting toes)
- Imagination (pretending the tambourine is a hat, dish, guitar, and so on)
- Improvisation and creative thinking
- Kinesthetic awareness (feeling the tambourine on the palm, head, arm, elbow, and so on)
- Social skills (sharing ideas and respecting those of others)

Here are some of my favorite pieces (available via online music-purchasing sites) to play along to in free-improvisation sessions with tambourines:

- "Gazooba," *Gazooba!* by Kinderjazz
- "Siyahamba," *Drum Like an Animal* by Tom Foote
- "Mexican Hat Dance," *All-Time Favorite Dances* from Kimbo Educational
- "McNamara's Band" (instrumental version), *Preschool Playtime Band* from Kimbo Educational

Activities Using Drums

The drum is one of the earliest known instruments in human history. Almost every culture on earth has used drums in ceremonies, rituals, and entertainment. The drum holds a central role in human cultures, and drumming activities will enrich any early childhood music program. If you look at a young child's face when she is drumming, you will see how deeply satisfying it is for children to bang on a drum.

Many beautiful and well-made children's drums are available; however, most of them are rather expensive and impractical to purchase for every child in the classroom. Coffee cans make a wonderful substitute. In fact, they are suitable for playing in large groups because their sound is softer and more muted than most commercially made drums. Another musical advantage is that coffee cans can be turned upside down and played on the metal side for a different sound, which encourages auditory discrimination and improvisational flexibility.

You may wish to make a class project out of collecting coffee cans and decorating them with paint, construction paper, crayons, or other materials. This makes the drums more individual, and children enjoy taking out their own drums when it is music time. Be aware, though, that paint and paper will change the sound of the instrument—uncovered metal has a sharper, brighter sound.

Another plus is that coffee cans are familiar household objects to most children. When I bring one out, someone is sure to say, "My mom drinks coffee!" or "We have coffee at my house!" very excitedly. It starts a meaningful, engaging conversation among the children. Using coffee cans to make music promotes the idea of repurposing objects rather than throwing them away. I always tell my students that before I throw anything away, I ask myself, "Could I make music with this?" The answer is often yes, and I have overflowing bags of "musical junk" in my closet to prove it.

One helpful tip: Before you pass out coffee cans to the group, bring one out, and ask the children to guess what is inside it. Then remove the lid to show them—it is empty! So, there is no need for them to open it up themselves. This reduces the number of children who take off the lids in the middle of an activity and then cannot get them back on. (A few will try this anyway.) Some crafty teachers use glue to secure the lid to the can; you might want to try that, too.

Pitter-Patter

Here is a fun activity for a rainy day.

1. Lightly tap your drum with all the fingertips of one hand, and sing softly to the tune of "Frère Jacques":
   Pitter-patter, pitter-patter,
   Hear the rain? Hear the rain?
   Pitter-patter, pitter-patter,
   That's the rain. That's the rain.

2. Sing the second verse:
   Raining harder, raining harder, (pat with flat hand)
   Hear the rain? Hear the rain?
   Raining harder, raining harder,
   That's the rain. That's the rain.

3. Sing the third verse:
   Even harder, even harder, (pat with both hands,
       alternating left-right, quickly)
   Hear the rain? Hear the rain?
   Even harder, even harder,
   That's the rain. That's the rain.

4. Sing the fourth verse :
   Boom, boom, thunder! Boom, boom, thunder! (pound
       drum with fist)
   It's a storm! It's a storm!
   Boom, boom, thunder! Boom, boom, thunder!
   It's a storm! It's a storm!

5. Sing the fifth verse:
   Rain is stopping, rain is stopping, (tap lightly with
       fingertips, getting slower and lighter until the last
       line, when rain stops)
   Almost gone, almost gone,
   Rain is stopping, rain is stopping,
   Now it's gone. Now it's gone.

LEARNING BENEFITS

- Curiosity
- Fine-motor skills
- Imagination (acting out raindrops dropping)
- Preliteracy—sequence (in the song, the storm grows in strength and then subsides)
- Science (harder force creates louder sounds, lighter force creates quieter sounds)

Boom on My Little Drum

Even toddlers can enjoy this simple activity that explores different ways to make sounds on the drum.

LEARNING BENEFITS

- Curiosity
- Fine-motor skills
- Improvisation and creative thinking
- Science (forceful touches such as pounding make louder sounds, lighter touches such as scratching make quieter sounds)
- Social skills (sharing ideas and respecting those of others)

1. First, pound on the drum with your fist, and sing to the tune of "The Old Gray Mare":
   This is how I boom on my little drum,
   Boom on my little drum, boom on my little drum,
   This is how I boom on my little drum,
   Can you boom like me?

2. Additional verses:
   This is how I knock on my little drum... (knock on the drum with knuckles)
   This is how I pat on my little drum... (pat with hand)
   This is how I tap on my little drum... (tap with one finger)
   This is how I scratch on my little drum... (scratch with fingernails)

3. Ask the children if there are any other ways they could play on their little drums.

Do You Know the Tap, Tap, Tap?

This easy and fun activity includes a preschool favorite: the sudden loud noise after a period of quiet. Young children are excellent at being loud!

1. Tap one finger on the drum, and sing to the tune of "Do You Know the Muffin Man?":
   Do you know the tap, tap, tap,
   The tap, tap, tap, the tap, tap, tap,
   Do you know the tap, tap, tap,
   The tap, tap, tap, tap, tap? BOOM! (On *BOOM!*
       pound on the drum with your fist and shout!)
2. Additional verses:
   Do you know the knock, knock, knock? (knock on the
       drum with knuckles)
   Do you know the pat, pat, pat?... (pat the drum with
       flat hand)
   Do you know the scratch, scratch, scratch?...
       (scratch the drum with fingernails while singing
       very quietly)
3. Have the children think of other ways to play the
   drum before shouting, "BOOM!"

LEARNING BENEFITS

- Auditory memory
  (remembering the auditory
  cue to shout, "BOOM!")
- Curiosity
- Fine-motor skills
- Improvisation and creative
  thinking
- Listening skills (listening for
  the end of the song to shout,
  "BOOM!")
- Social skills (sharing ideas
  and respecting those of
  others)

Tap-a-Doodle-Doo

Children love the word *tap-a-doodle-doo* and the other *-a-doodle-doo* words. Maybe they remind them of the rooster's "cock-a-doodle-doo." At any rate, they enjoy singing along with the silly words in this activity.

LEARNING BENEFITS

- Curiosity (exploring music and instruments)
- Fine-motor skills
- Improvisation and creative thinking
- Phonemic awareness (putting different words together with "-a-doodle-doo")
- Social skills

1. Tap on the drum with one finger, and sing to the tune of "Jimmy Crack Corn":

   This is how I tap-a-doodle-doo,
   This is how I tap-a-doodle-doo,
   This is how I tap-a-doodle-doo,
   I tap-a-doodle, tap-a-doodle-doo!

2. Additional verses:

   This is how I knock-a-doodle-doo... (knock on the drum with knuckles)

   This is how I flick-a-doodle-doo... (hold your third finger with your thumb and release it to "flick" on the drum)

   This is how I pat-a-doodle-doo... (pat on the drum with your whole hand)

   This is how I thumb-a-doodle-doo... (tap on the drum with your thumb)

3. Invite the children to think up new ways to "doodle-doo" on the drum.

4. **Variation:** Children love thinking up new nonsense words. What would be another funny end to these words? Maybe "tappa-wappa-wham" or "tappa-deedle-dee?" Try these, and then ask the children if they can think of more funny word endings.

Free-Improvisation Ideas for Drums

Please see the section on "Free-Improvisation Ideas for Rhythm Sticks" for a discussion of the benefits of free improvisation and suggestions on how to lead a session.

Try these different techniques to inspire children's creative thinking with the drums.

- Turn the drum upside down and tap it
- Tap it while holding it sideways on the floor
- Roll it sideways on the floor
- Hold it on top of your head and tap it
- Tap the head of the drum while holding the drum between your feet
- Tap the sides of the drum
- Lightly tap it with fingertips
- Tap it with your thumb
- Tap it with your elbow
- Tap it with your nose
- Hold the drum and thump it on the floor
- Use your two pointer fingers like drumsticks

Here are some of my favorite pieces (available via online music-purchasing sites) to play along to in free-improvisation sessions with drums:

- "Old McDonald Had a Farm," *A Tisket, a Tasket, a Child's Rhythm Basket* by Brent Lewis
- "March of the Wooden Soldiers," *Pre-K Hooray* from Kimbo Educational
- "Drum Like an Animal," *Drum Like an Animal* by Tom Foote
- "Mardi Gras Mambo," *Fire on the Bayou* by the Meters

LEARNING BENEFITS

- Curiosity
- Directionality (playing the drum upside down and sideways)
- Fine-motor skills
- Improvisation and creative thinking
- Kinesthetic awareness (feeling the drum with head, elbow, feet, and so on)
- Social skills (sharing ideas and respecting those of others)

Activities Using Other Rhythm Instruments

Playing the Xylophone

The xylophone is actually one of my favorite instruments for young children. It is one of the only pitched instruments they can play effectively and with some understanding of how the tones are related. Also, its structure is similar to a piano—in fact, you could say it is almost like an introduction to the piano keyboard.

I recommend xylophones that are small, with removable metal bars—the sound is bright, cheerful, and appealing to young children. Some of these xylophones also have the names of the notes of the C scale (C-D-E-F-G-A-B-C) on the bars. Children are excited to recognize the letters, and this is an easy, age-appropriate way to introduce them to the idea that musical notes have letter names.

I do not recommend xylophones that have the metal bars rising up diagonally from low notes to high notes. This promotes a misconception that high notes are physically higher than low notes. Actually, high notes are made by smaller vibrations and, therefore, by smaller objects than low notes.

1. Because of the expense and the relatively complex task of playing the xylophone, I use only one xylophone in a session. I play it, and then each student takes a turn. I teach many concepts using this instrument. It can be played loudly, like a stomping elephant, or lightly, like a skittering mouse. It can be played in a "running" way, like the hare, or in a slow "walk," like the tortoise. You can also make what I call the "magic sound" by quickly and lightly sweeping the mallet across the keys in a glissando—it really does sound magical, and children love it.

2. You will want to stay near each child as he plays the xylophone to ensure his safety and help him if he needs to replace bars that might come

off during too-enthusiastic playing. However, with supervision, the xylophone is an excellent way to introduce musical concepts in an enjoyable way.

3. **Variation:** Another interesting way to play the xylophone is to use what is known as the pentatonic, or five-note, scale. By removing the F and B bars, you have a five-note scale (C-D-E-G-A, with another C at the top). When children play notes in this scale, even randomly, the notes will harmonize well with each other and produce a nice melody. The pentatonic scale is widely used in the Orff approach to music education. Four- and five-year-olds can definitely understand the idea that some notes go with each other better than other notes, and they enjoy making up their own melodies. You could even give them two mallets at a time for them to experiment with harmony (two or more notes played together).

LEARNING BENEFITS
- Curiosity
- Fine-motor skills
- Imagination (pretending to play as animals would)
- Improvisation and creative thinking
- Musical awareness (high and low notes, harmony)
- Social skills (sharing ideas and respecting those of others)

Playing the Ukulele

Young children love playing the ukulele. As they grow from toddlerhood through kindergarten age, they will try playing it in many different ways. I recommend purchasing a small, inexpensive ukulele. The most important issues are safety and durability, not perfect sound quality.

LEARNING BENEFITS

- Curiosity
- Fine-motor skills (strumming and plucking strings)
- Improvisation and creative thinking
- Social skills (sharing ideas and respecting those of others)

1. As with the xylophone, I bring in one ukulele to class, and we take turns exploring the many ways to play it.

2. I begin by showing children how to strum all the strings by brushing the backs of my fingertips across the strings or by just brushing my thumb lightly across them. (Young children generally prefer the thumb method.) I also show them how to pluck the strings separately.

   Some children will try both strumming and plucking; some will stick to one or the other. Some toddlers and two-year-olds will just hit the strings with their hands. Many will hold the instrument flat across the lap rather than in the traditional way. That is okay—I never correct a small child's technique. This is a time for exploring and investigating, not perfecting technique.

3. Older children often like to sing a song, one they know or one they improvise on the spot, while they play. I always worry that other children will get impatient for their turn, but generally they love to hear each other perform and will listen attentively. The ukulele brings out a lot of creativity and a poetic use of language. It is really a wonderful instrument for young children.

Playing the Guiro

The guiro is one of the oldest percussion instruments, dating back to the pre-Columbian era. "Real" guiros are carved from hollowed-out gourds, but most children's guiros are made of wood. I have seen them in a variety of shapes, including animals such as fish and frogs. Some guiros have handles, which are easier for young children to play.

The guiro is played by scraping a stick along parallel notches cut into the sides of the instrument. This gives it its characteristic rasping sound. A roomful of children playing guiros would be pretty ear splitting, so this is another instrument I have the children play one at a time.

1. Demonstrate how to play the guiro, emphasizing that it requires a pretty strong scrape to get a nice sound. The wooden frog guiros should be held with the head facing out and then played tail to head.

2. **Variation:** Another fun use for the guiro is to make it portray a frog in a read-aloud book. With its croaky rasp, it adds fun and flavor to the story. If you have one child playing the guiro this way, be sure to take time afterward to pass the guiro around so each child has an opportunity to explore this unique instrument.

LEARNING BENEFITS
- Curiosity
- Fine-motor skills (scraping the guiro)
- Imagination (pretending the sound of the guiro is a frog croaking)
- Improvisation and creative thinking
- Social skills (sharing ideas and respecting those of others)

Playing the Triangle

Triangles are included in just about every rhythm-band set for young children, but for many years I did not know why they were considered appropriate for this age group. For one thing, the older style of triangle required a lot coordination and control to play successfully. In addition, the triangle's sound is not only loud, but it is also probably the brightest, sharpest sound in the percussion family. It actually is disturbing to some children. (I have seen some cover their ears.)

Today, although I still feel that a little bit of triangle goes a long way, I think it is worth using once in a while to introduce the children to its unique sound and structure. The newer style of triangle is much easier to play. In the past, triangles had a separate string loop to hold the instrument, and while a child was busy negotiating the string, the triangle itself would often fall out, leaving the child frustrated and upset. The newer style has a string holder attached to the triangle through a hole in the top of the instrument. A child can slip his finger through the string, and the triangle will stay put, making it much easier to hit with the striker.

LEARNING BENEFITS

- Curiosity
- Fine-motor skills
- Improvisation and creative thinking
- Science (learning how to stop sound by holding the triangle tightly, discovering that metal instruments make very bright sounds)
- Social skills (sharing ideas and respecting those of others)

1. Show the children how the triangle can be played loudly or softly, depending on how hard it is hit. Also demonstrate that holding the triangle itself stops the sound, and the instrument will not make the distinctive "ding."
2. Pass the triangle around for each child to play.
3. For younger children, it can be helpful to just hold the triangle and have them hit it with the striker. A puppet can also hold the triangle for them; toddlers love to play music with a puppet.

Playing the Lollipop Drum

The lollipop drum is a popular children's instrument. It consists of a simple frame drum with a pretuned drumhead and a long handle, making it suitable for young children. It is played by hitting it with a mallet that has a soft foam-rubber head. The lollipop drum is fairly expensive, however, so I only bring in one at a time to explore with a class.

The lollipop drum comes in three different sizes, with 6-inch, 8-inch, and 10-inch diameters. I usually use the 6-inch drum because it is the most accessible for all of my students, even the littlest ones. It can be interesting, however, to have an older group compare the differences in pitch among the three sizes.

1. Demonstrate the traditional way to play, hitting the drum on the lollipop side.

2. Wonder aloud if it will sound the same if you play it turned around, on the white side. Let everyone guess, and then show them that it does, indeed, sound the same on the white side.

3. Clasp the side of the drumhead to stop the head from vibrating, and ask the same question—will it sound the same or different? Many children are surprised to hear how different it sounds. This is a good introduction to the idea of making hypotheses and testing them.

4. When you pass the instrument around, the children will often get very creative with it, playing it loudly or almost inaudibly, hitting the handle with the mallet, or even hitting the mallet with the handle! They also like to hide their faces behind the drum, tap it lightly, and then remove the drum to peek out. It is amazing how creative children can be in an atmosphere that encourages free exploration.

LEARNING BENEFITS
- Curiosity
- Fine-motor skills
- Improvisation and creative thinking
- Science (stopping the sound by holding the drumhead tightly)
- Social skills (sharing ideas and respecting those of others)

Shake, Rattle, and Roll

PART TWO:
Music and Movement Activities and Games

HOW MUSIC AND MOVEMENT ACTIVITIES HELP CHILDREN LEARN AND GROW

Four-year-old DeAndre never just walks or runs into a room. He enters dancing, with a funky exuberance, twirling and stomping, his elbows and knees jerking and twisting in all directions. It always makes me smile to see his fun and totally unselfconscious dance moves.

They are not all as outgoing or boisterous as DeAndre, but all young children are natural movers, This makes sense because they are developing their growing muscles and learning about their bodies' capabilities and possibilities. They run, they climb, they jump, they reach—they do just about everything except sit. So, why do we need to concern ourselves with providing physical activities for young children?

First of all, we need to be sure that young children are mastering specific developmental tasks. They should be able to kick, hop, tiptoe, walk along a line, balance on only one foot, and jump over very short barriers.

Secondly, our culture of TV, video games, cell phones, and other screens is encroaching on the physical play time of even very young children. The Centers for Disease Control and Prevention

recommends that young children and adolescents do sixty minutes or more of physical activity every day, including aerobic activity, muscle strengthening (such as gymnastics), and bone strengthening (such as jump rope or running). Many young children do not achieve even close to this amount of time. A study by Kristen Copeland and colleagues found that children spend only 2 to 3 percent of their time doing vigorous physical activity during an eight-hour day in child care.

So, how do we get more physical activity into the young child's day? We cannot spend all day playing on the playground, and besides, many school days are too cold, hot, or rainy for children to be outside for long. That is where music and movement activities come in!

Movement is a natural response to music. In fact, music and dance have been linked since the beginning of recorded history. Moving seems to connect us to music in a unique way, engaging our bodies and minds in making sense of the rhythms and melodies. But, why do we like to dance to music?

There is no one clear answer. Scientists have found that music activates the cerebellum, which is also involved in the coordination and timing of movement. This is a connection but not a causal relationship. Possibly, we want to move to music because the beat seems to demand a rhythmic response. When we listen to songs with a strong beat, it is almost like we cannot help dancing or at least tapping our feet! Young children, even babies, engage in rhythmic movement or dancing when exposed to rhythmic music. And rhythmic movement to music benefits young children's development across many domains.

■ **Health and physical development.** Moving to music is an aerobic activity that helps children maintain a healthy weight, increases stamina, activates the immune system, strengthens the heart, and keeps muscles strong. Movements such as jumping and running in place also help bones stay strong and healthy.

We are all aware of the obesity epidemic in this country, which is affecting more and more children every year. Music and movement activities are an enjoyable way to get young children in the habit of physical activity and to help prevent weight problems.

In addition, movement activities give young children the opportunity to practice motor skills such as stretching their arms, bending and unbending their knees, swaying their hips, shrugging their shoulders, kicking, marching, tiptoeing, galloping, jumping, and hopping on one foot. Movement activities support all areas of physical coordination, posture, body awareness, and spatial awareness.

■ **Social development.** For thousands of years, moving to music in a group has been used to help people bond together. In religious and tribal rituals, in military drills, in any situation where it is desirable to form a cohesive group, people have moved to music. We have done this throughout human history for the simple reason that it works. Think of how you feel at a wedding or other social gathering when you dance to music in a large group. You feel happier, more comfortable, and more connected to the group, right? Dancing in a circle enhances this feeling of connectedness. Many traditional group dances, such as the hora, are performed in a circle, with dancers often holding hands and seeing all the other members of the group.

For young children, away from their homes, who need the comfort and security of belonging to a group, moving to music is a wonderful, playful, fun social-bonding experience. It is hard not to smile and laugh while dancing in a group, especially to a happy or humorous song. And, sharing smiles connects children to each other like nothing else.

■ **Emergent literacy.** As early-childhood expert Rae Pica states, "There are many links between literacy and movement. Movement and language are both forms of communication and self-expression." Music and movement activities promote many skills used in language and literacy. Moving to music often depends on interpreting auditory signals, such as stopping and freezing in place when the music stops. Many songs also support auditory memory. For instance, children may need to remember to pat their heads when they hear the word *hat*. Movement songs introduce new words to help build children's vocabulary. Learning words such as *soft*, *strong, sway,* and *wiggle* is more meaningful to young children when they are both hearing the word and feeling the sense of the word.

- **Musical concepts.** Music and movement activities use a multisensory approach to introduce musical concepts. Children hear the teacher talk about a concept, such as fast and slow clapping; they see their teacher demonstrate it; and they do fast and slow clapping themselves, feeling the difference in their bodies. The involvement of many senses strengthens and reinforces their learning.

  Musical concepts introduced in these activities include soft and loud; getting softer and getting louder; fast and slow; getting faster and getting slower; legato and staccato (smooth and connected versus jerky, unconnected sounds and movements); timbre (sound quality, taught by exploring sounds made by different parts of the body); and keeping a steady beat, using hands, feet, or other body parts.

- **Math.** As discussed in the previous section, the beat in music is a division of time. In any given piece of music, all beats are equal in duration. Although it would not be developmentally appropriate to teach concepts such as equal parts and duration, it is very appropriate to introduce these ideas in ways children hear, see, and feel in their bodies.

  In many of the activities in this section, we keep the steady beat by clapping, patting thighs, stomping, walking in place, running in place, tapping our heads and other parts of the body, and as many other ways as the children can think of. We also keep the beat by waving scarves and bouncing beanie animals.

  Exposure to patterns is also central to many of these activities. Beats in music are arranged in patterns called *measures,* or *bars.* The activities in this section use beat patterns of 1-2-3-4, 1-2-3-4; or 1-2-3, 1-2-3. These patterns are emphasized by playing a slightly stronger beat on 1 and by the words of the song (for example, *IT-sy*). Note that the parentheses indicate a beat with no words accompanying it. Therefore, to maintain the pattern, children should clap or tap on that beat. For instance, the beat pattern of "The Itsy Bitsy Spider" would look like this:

	1	2	3	4
The	itsy	bitsy	spi-	der

	1	2	3	(4)
Went up the	*water*	*spout.*	(clap)	

1	2	3	4
Down	*came the*	*rain*	*and*

1	2	3	(4)
Washed the spider	*out!*	(clap)	

Singing the words while clapping on all the numbered beats will make the beat pattern clearer.

Also, the children's movements themselves are often arranged in patterns. We might tap our shoulders during the first three lines of a song and clap on the fourth line. This would be an AAAB pattern. Or, there might be a song with two alternating sections in which we walk in place during one section and run in place during the other section. This would be an ABAB pattern. Patterning is a basic concept in both music and math.

■ **Emotional development.** Oops—I almost forgot something really important about music and movement activities. They are fun! Dancing and moving around to music feels good. Feeling the beat, stomping your feet, shaking your hips, bouncing, and jumping while listening to music is one of the best stress relievers ever. When moving to music we feel happy, energized, and relaxed at the same time.

Young children need these kinds of activities every day. Rambunctious children need them to let off steam and release pent-up energy. Shy, quiet children need to let loose in a safe environment and to gain confidence. All young children need music and movement to let go of the stresses and worries of the day. With movement and music activities, they can be as playful and silly as they want and can express their individuality freely.

Which makes me think of DeAndre again. If just thinking about his joyful, energetic movement makes me smile, imagine how good it must make him feel to do it! The joy of moving to music makes every day happier, and when children are happy, they are ready to learn.

Activities about Body Parts

Young children are still learning about the parts of the body. Hearing about them is good. Seeing illustrations of body-part words in books is better. But, children learn about body parts most effectively by actually moving the body parts while they hear and sing the words. For instance, if a child hears and sings the word *arm* while shaking her arm, the learning is reinforced by using all three modalities. Her understanding and memory of the word *arm* will be much greater than it would be by simply hearing the word *arm.*

Clappety-Clap

I like to use this kind of easy, improvisatory activity to begin a music session. It gets children moving and energized and gets their minds energized, too, thinking of new movements. It is also good for getting the wiggles out before we sit down to read a story or do a more challenging activity.

LEARNING BENEFITS

- Curiosity
- Fine-motor skills (clapping)
- Gross-motor skills (patting knees, jumping, kicking)
- Improvisation and creative thinking
- Patterns (pattern is clapping, patting, clapping, patting, clapping, patting, clapping— an ABABABA pattern)
- Social skills (sharing ideas and respecting those of others)

1. Children should be standing in a circle. Explain to them that this is a clapping song but that they are going to clap in a special rhythm—"clap-pet-y clap," with one clap per syllable. Practice this rhythmic clap a few times.

2. Clap and move as indicated in the song, while singing to the tune of "Jimmy Crack Corn":
   Clappety-clap and pat your knees,
   Clappety-clap and pat your knees,
   Clappety-clap and pat your knees,
   And clappety-clap again.

3. Additional verses:
   Clappety-clap and jump up and down...
   Clappety-clap and kick your feet...

4. Then comes the fun part—ask the children to think of other movements we could do after we "clappety-clap." They will love to come up with inventive and fun ideas.

Tap Your Shoulders

Start out with tapping in this activity, but you do not have to limit yourself to tapping motions—you can tickle, scratch, and pat other body parts. It is an easy improvisational activity.

1. Children should be standing in a circle. Gently tap your shoulders while singing to the tune of "Oh My Darling, Clementine":

   Tap your shoulders, tap your shoulders,
   Tap your shoulders, tap, tap, tap,
   Tap your shoulders, tap your shoulders,
   Tap your shoulders, tap, tap, tap.

2. Additional verses:

   Tap your knees, tap your knees,
   Tap your knees, tap, tap, tap,
   Tap your knees, tap your knees,
   Tap your knees, tap, tap, tap.
   Tap your ears...
   Tap your hips...

LEARNING BENEFITS

- Curiosity
- Fine-motor skills (tapping, tickling, scratching)
- Improvisation and creative thinking
- Kinesthetic awareness (feeling hands and fingers on different parts of the body)
- Social skills (sharing ideas and respecting those of others)

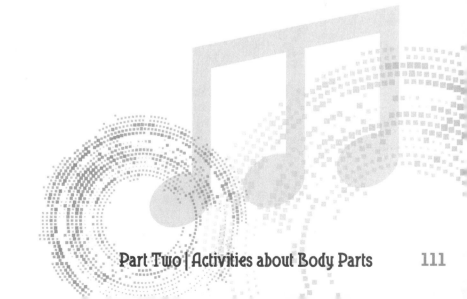

'Round, 'Round, All Around

It seems like many movement activities for young children are based on linear movement such as jumping, stretching, or moving from head to toe. This activity is based on circular movement for a nice change. You can ask children about other things that move in a circle (for instance, wheels and merry-go-rounds).

LEARNING BENEFITS

- Curiosity
- Fine-motor skills (moving fingers, hands, thumb)
- Gross-motor skills (moving arms and so on)
- Improvisation and creative thinking
- Math (exploring the circle shape)
- Social skills (sharing ideas and respecting those of others)

1. Children should be standing in a circle. Move your pointer fingers in circles and sing to the tune of "Row, Row, Row Your Boat":
   'Round, 'round, all around,
   Fingers making circles,
   'Round, 'round, all around,
   Fingers making circles.

2. Then move your hands in circles:
   'Round, 'round, all around,
   Hands are making circles,
   'Round, 'round, all around,
   Hands are making circles.

3. Additional verses:
   ...Arms are making circles...
   ...Thumbs are making circles...

4. This activity can be expanded to other body parts, such as shoulders, legs, a foot, or even elbows. If the children move their heads in circles, remind them to do this slowly and carefully.

Did You Ever See Your Fingers?

This activity is based on the old song "Did You Ever See a Lassie?" I like the lilting tune, and it lends itself to the side-to-side movement of this activity.

1. Ask the children if they can move their fluttering fingers from side to side in a gently swinging motion (demonstrate it for them). Then when everyone is comfortable with the motion, add the song to the tune of "Did You Ever See a Lassie?":

   Did you ever see your fingers go this way and that way?

   Did you ever see your fingers go this way and that?

   Go this way and that way, go this way and that way.

   Did you ever see your fingers go this way and that?

2. Additional verses:

   ...your foot...

   ...your arms...

   ...your leg...

3. Have the children decide on other body parts to go "this way and that."

4. **Variation:** Instead of moving side to side, on "this way and that" you could move your fingers or other body parts up and down or forward and back.

LEARNING BENEFITS

- Curiosity
- Directionality (left and right)
- Gross-motor skills (swaying arms and legs)
- Improvisation and creative thinking
- Social skills (sharing ideas and respecting those of others)

The Tickle Bugs

Watch out! The tickle bugs are here, and they are tickling you everywhere!

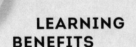

LEARNING BENEFITS

- Curiosity
- Fine-motor skills (tickling)
- Improvisation and creative thinking
- Kinesthetic awareness (feeling fingers on head, shoulders, elbows)
- Social skills (sharing ideas and respecting those of others)

1. Children should be standing in a circle. Use both hands to be "tickle bugs" with wiggly legs (your fingers), and tickle your head while singing to the tune of "If You're Happy and You Know It":

   Oh, the tickle bugs are tickling your head,
   Oh, the tickle bugs are tickling your head,
   And no matter what you say, (spread out hands, palms up)
   They will never go away, (shake your head side to side as if saying no)
   Oh, the tickle bugs are tickling your head! (tickle head again)

2. Additional verses:

   Oh, the tickle bugs are tickling your shoulders...
   ...your elbows...
   ...your knees...

Activities about Animals

Most young children love to pretend to be animals. Part of the fun of this kind of play is the opportunity to explore physical movement—hopping like frogs, flapping their wings like chickens, stomping like elephants, and other motions. For instance, instead of just hopping, pretending to be a *frog* hopping captures the child's imagination and makes the experience more engaging.

The Penguin Dance

What is it about penguins? Their black-and-white tuxedo elegance? Their charming waddle? Their exotic habitat in the South Pole? Whatever it is, the penguin seems to be a popular animal. This dance gives young children the opportunity to pretend to be these endearing creatures.

Do the penguin dance to the music of "The Syncopated Clock" by Leroy Anderson. (This piece is featured on the CD *Kids Can Listen, Kids Can Move!* by Lynn Kleiner. It is also available separately via online music-purchasing sites.) The music is meant to sound like a ticking clock, and it does, but it also reminds me of a penguin's waddling gait.

LEARNING BENEFITS

- Curiosity
- Gross-motor skills (waddling, turning, flapping)
- Imagination (pretending to be a penguin)
- Improvisation and creative thinking
- Social skills (sharing ideas and respecting those of others)

1. Start out waddling in place to the beat.
2. After a while, lead the children in turning around (while still waddling), jumping while flapping their flippers (also known as arms), swimming with their flippers, diving into the water (still standing), and catching a fish and eating it.
3. You may add other movements or ask the children to think of some.
4. **Variation:** When the children are familiar with this activity, they can take turns being the leader and choosing motions for the others to copy.

Old MacDonald's Bugs

I like to use this activity in summer when children start to notice the bugs outside. (Sometimes inside, too!) It is fun to read a story about bugs and then continue the bug fun with this activity.

1. Choose two children to be the bugs in each verse. They will act out their parts in the middle of the circle while the class sings to the tune of "Old MacDonald":
   Old MacDonald had a farm, E-I-E-I-O,
   And on his farm he had some grasshoppers,
   *   E-I-E-I-O,*
   With a hop-hop here and a hop-hop there,
   Here a hop, there a hop, everywhere a hop-hop,
   Old MacDonald had a farm, E-I-E-I-O.

2. Additional verses:
   ...And on his farm he had some flies (fly-fly)...
   ...worms (wiggle-wiggle)...
   ...butterflies (flutter-flutter)...
   ...ants (crawl-crawl)...
   and even
   ...mosquitoes (bite-bite)...
   if you can trust your students not to really bite!

3. Instead of showing your students how to make "correct" movements, ask them how they think that bug would move. If you have a large space, more children can act out each bug.

LEARNING BENEFITS

- Curiosity
- Gross-motor skills (crawling, hopping, wiggling)
- Imagination (pretending to be bugs)
- Improvisation and creative thinking
- Social skills (moving in the center of the circle with another child while respecting her space)

Kangaroos

This is a great activity for the beginning of the year, when you and the children are learning each other's names. This gives you a fun and very bouncy way to do it!

LEARNING BENEFITS

- Curiosity
- Imagination (pretending to be kangaroos)
- Listening skills (listening for their names to join the "kangaroos")
- Locomotor skills (jumping around the inside of the circle)

1. Choose two children to be kangaroos. They will jump around in the middle of the circle while the class claps to the beat and sings to the tune of "Jingle Bells":

   Kangaroos, kangaroos, jumping kangaroos,
   Kangaroos, kangaroos, jumping kangaroos!

2. Then sing to the tune of the "Dashing through the snow" part:

   One day these kangaroos,
   Met another kangaroo,
   A very nice kangaroo,
   Her name was Sahasra Roo! (name a child in the circle, who will jump up and join the other jumping kangaroos)

3. Continue until the circle is full. Continue playing if more children need turns to be kangaroos!

The Parrots Fly in the Jungle

So many children's books take place in the jungle, I wanted a fun movement song that would be flexible enough to include all the animals that appear in each story. In this activity, children pretend to be different jungle animals and act out their movements.

1. Ask for two children to be parrots. They will go to the middle of the circle and "fly" around while the class sings to the tune of "The Bear Went over the Mountain":

   The parrots fly in the jungle,
   The parrots fly in the jungle,
   The parrots fly in the jungle,
   They fly and fly and fly!

2. Then ask for two tigers that prowl in the jungle.
3. Additional verses:

   The elephants stomp in the jungle...
   The monkeys swing in the jungle...
   The frogs jump in the jungle...

4. Continue with other jungle animals the children may suggest.
5. **Variation:** This activity could be about other animals and their habitats, such as forest animals ("The bears stomp in the forest") or farm animals ("The horses gallop on the farm").

LEARNING BENEFITS

- Curiosity
- Imagination (pretending to be animals)
- Improvisation and creative thinking
- Locomotor skills (flying, stomping, swinging, and so on)
- Patterns (the first three lines of each verse have the same words; the fourth is different—an AAAB pattern)
- Social skills (moving inside the circle with other children while respecting their space)

A Little Cat

This activity, like several others in this section, uses my "special pretending blanket"—a small cotton blanket children can hide under in pretending games. (For toddlers and two-year-olds, I sometimes drape the blanket over their heads just a bit so they can still see out, since some of them are uncomfortable being unable to see.)

LEARNING BENEFITS

- Auditory memory (remembering musical cues)
- Curiosity
- Gross-motor skills (popping out of the blanket)
- Imagination (pretending to be a cat)
- Listening skills (listening for cues to meow and to pop out)

1. Choose one child at a time to be a "cat" who hides under the blanket while the class claps to the beat and sings to the tune of "Polly Wolly Doodle":
   A little cat named Jessica
   Is hiding in the house,
   But if we say, "Meow, meow,"
   Then maybe she'll come out!

2. The class then calls, "Meow, meow," and the "cat" pops up out of the blanket.

3. This game is a good tie-in to stories about cats. You can also substitute another small animal for a cat, depending on the story or unit you are exploring that day.

Flies in the Buttermilk

For some reason, I have found that young children love to pretend to be flies—maybe it is an acceptable way to let off some steam and get their "buzziness" out.

1. This activity begins with the group singing "Skip to My Lou" in the traditional way while clapping to the beat. Then choose two children to be flies that fly and buzz around the middle of the circle while you sing:
   Flies in the buttermilk, shoo, fly, shoo,
   Flies in the buttermilk, shoo, fly, shoo,
   Flies in the buttermilk, shoo, fly, shoo,
   Skip to my Lou, my darlin'.

2. You can continue with more children taking turns to be flies. Or, you may decide (or the children may decide for you) that it would be fun to have other animals in the buttermilk—even frogs, bunnies, or bears.

LEARNING BENEFITS
- Curiosity
- Fine-motor skills (clapping)
- Imagination (pretending to be flies and other animals)
- Improvisation and creative thinking
- Locomotor skills ("flying" and performing other movements inside the circle)
- Patterns (the first three lines of each verse have the same words; the fourth line is different—an AAAB pattern)
- Social skills (sharing ideas and respecting those of others)

Sing a Song of Sixpence

This activity has been one of my students' favorites for years. It has a silly premise (birds singing in a pie) and a popping-out surprise at the end for extra fun.

LEARNING BENEFITS

- Auditory memory (remembering auditory cues)
- Curiosity
- Imagination (pretending to be birds and other animals)
- Improvisation and creative thinking
- Listening skills (waiting for the song to end to pop up and sing)
- Social skills (hiding under a blanket with another child while respecting his space)

1. Teach the song to the class, using the traditional tune:
   Sing a song of sixpence, a pocket full of rye,
   Four-and-twenty blackbirds baked in a pie,
   When the pie was opened, the birds began to sing,
   And wasn't that a dainty dish to set before the king!

2. I have found that defining all the old-fashioned words in this nursery rhyme takes a while and makes the children tend to lose focus. Instead, you can just ask them, "Did you hear what was in the pie?" and "What did the birds do when the people opened up the pie?" At that point, they can practice singing like birds.

3. Then comes the game. Choose two or three children at a time to be the birds, and cover them with a "piecrust" (a small blanket). Have the class sing the song while clapping to the beat, and then lift up the piecrust and have the "birds" pop up and sing. They will be greeted by applause and laughter!

4. **Variation:** When the children know the activity well, open it up to improvisation. Let the children decide what animals they would like to be in the pie. When you "open the pie," they can make the appropriate sound. I have had pies with pigs, ducks, and even tigers.

Hop, Hop, Hopping

I usually pretend frogs are hop, hop, hopping in this activity, but you could just as easily use bunnies or even kangaroos!

1. Choose two children to be frogs. Explain that during the activity, you will say another child's name, and that child will jump in the circle and join the other frogs.

2. The two frogs jump around inside the circle while the class claps to the beat and chants:
   Two little froggies went hop, hop, hopping,
   Along came Jared, and they kept on hopping.
   They hopped and they hopped until they stopped!

3. On *stopped*, the frogs should stop and freeze but remain in the circle.

4. Repeat until there are five or six frogs—that is usually plenty. Then, start again with new frogs!

LEARNING BENEFITS
- Curiosity
- Imagination (pretending to be frogs)
- Listening skills (waiting for their names to be called, listening for verbal cue to stop hopping)
- Locomotor skills (hopping around inside of the circle)
- Rhythmic awareness (strong rhythm in chanting)
- Social skills (hopping around inside the circle with other children while respecting one another's space)

There's a Little Mouse in My House

Because there are so many children's books about mice, I am always trying to come up with more songs and games featuring the little creatures. This is one that engages the children.

LEARNING BENEFITS

- Curiosity
- Gross-motor skills (throwing and catching)
- Listening skills (listening for voice and position of "mouse," waiting for the end of the song to open eyes and guess)
- Social skills (taking turns)

1. Choose one child to sit in the middle of the circle and close his eyes. Give this child a small, soft ball to be the "cheese." Then silently point to a child sitting in the circle to be the "mouse."

2. Sing to the tune of "Hurry, Hurry, Drive the Fire Truck":

   There's a little mouse living in my house,
   There's a little mouse living in my house,
   There's a little mouse living in my house,
   Where is the little mouse?

3. At the end of the song, the "mouse" should say, "Squeak squeak," in a high voice. Then the child in the middle (the "listener") gets to open his eyes and guess which child was the "mouse." When he guesses correctly, he can gently throw the "cheese" to the "mouse," who tries to catch it. The "mouse" gets to be the next "listener."

4. **Variation:** Make this activity about a different animal, perhaps one you just read a story about. The child in the middle could throw a "fly" to a "frog," a "bone" to a "dog," and so on.

Dinosaur Babies

Young children get very excited about dinosaurs and love to learn about and pretend to be them. In this activity, baby dinosaurs "hatch" and start to move. You can customize this activity by inserting *Apatosaurus* or *Tyrannosaurus rex* instead of *dinosaur*, if you happen to be studying a certain kind of dinosaur.

1. Sing to the tune of "Hush, Little Baby":
   Dinosaur babies wait in their eggs, (hold arms over head like egg)
   Dinosaur babies wait in their eggs,
   Dinosaur babies wait in their eggs,
   That's what dinosaur babies do.

2. Additional verses:
   Dinosaur babies crack their shells... (make little punching motions to crack open your "shell")
   Dinosaur babies look all around... (stretch up neck and look left and right)
   Dinosaur babies stomp their feet... (stand and stomp your feet)
   Dinosaur babies swish their tails... (hold hand in back to be "tail")
   If your dinosaur is an herbivore...
   Dinosaur babies eat some leaves... (stretch head up and out to eat "leaves")
   Dinosaur babies take a nap... (curl up on the floor and close your eyes as if napping)

LEARNING BENEFITS
- Curiosity
- Gross-motor skills (punching, stretching, stamping feet, and so on)
- Imagination (pretending to be dinosaurs)
- Science (learning about dinosaurs)

Stomp like an Elephant

This rhythmic chanting activity is a nice tie-in to stories about jungle animals. In this version, I use the animals in the story *Hiccups for Elephant* **by James Preller, but you can adapt the activity to include the animals in any jungle story.**

1. The children should be standing in a circle. Tell them that in this activity they will be acting like the jungle animals in the story but moving to a certain rhythm. If you have a large space or a small group, they may move around the room. Otherwise, it is probably best if they move in place.

2. Start by clapping on every syllable, and act out the animal motions as you slowly chant:

   This is the rhy-thm.
   This is the rhy-thm.
   This is the rhy-thm.
   One, two, three.

3. Continue without stopping:

   First came the elephant,
   He likes to stomp.
   Stomp like an elephant, (stomp to the beat)
   Stomp like an elephant,
   Stomp like an elephant,
   Stomp, stomp, stomp!

   Then came the monkey,
   He likes to swing.
   Grab a branch and (put up one hand, then the other, and "grab a branch")
   Swing, swing, swing.
   Swing like a monkey,
   Swing like a monkey,
   Swing like a monkey,
   Swing, swing, swing!

Then came the lion,
He likes to prowl.
Prowl like a lion, (stretch out one arm, then the
    other, with fingers like claws)
Prowl like a lion,
Prowl like a lion,
Prowl, prowl, prowl.

Then came the zebra,
He's kind of like a horse,
So we're going to gallop!
Gallop like a zebra, (gallop in place)
Gallop like a zebra,
Gallop like a zebra,
Gallop, gallop, gallop.

Then came the mousy,
He likes to crawl.
Crawl like a mousy, ("crawl" with hands tucked under
    in front of your chest; wiggle fingers)
Crawl like a mousy,
Crawl like a mousy,
Crawl, crawl, crawl.

Now clap like a person,
Clap like a person,
Clap like a person,
And then sit down!

LEARNING BENEFITS
- Curiosity
- Fine-motor skills (crawling)
- Gross-motor skills (stomping, swinging, galloping, prowling)
- Imagination (pretending to be animals)
- Listening skills (moving according to the words they hear)
- Rhythmic awareness (moving to a certain rhythm)

The Owl Chicken Bunny Song

Young children really enjoy this funny activity, which gets them moving in some very silly ways!

LEARNING BENEFITS

- Auditory memory (remembering previous animal movements)
- Curiosity
- Fine-motor skills (making "owl eyes")
- Gross-motor skills (flapping "wings," hopping, turning around)
- Imagination (pretending to move like different animals)

1. The children should be standing in a circle. Make circles around your eyes with your thumbs and cupped hands, bounce to the beat, and sing to the tune of "Buffalo Gals":
   Make big eyes like an owl today,
   An owl today, an owl today,
   Oh, make big eyes like an owl today,
   And turn yourself around! (turn around while keeping the "owl eyes")

2. Ask the children to keep the owl eyes by making their eyes big without their hands, and ask them to "flap their wings" like a chicken. Sing:
   Flap your wings like a chicken today, (with hands tucked in at the armpits, elbows out)
   A chicken today, a chicken today,
   Oh, flap your wings like a chicken today,
   And turn yourself around!

3. Now ask the children to keep the owl eyes and the flapping wings but also hop up and down like a bunny! Sing:
   Hop up and down like a bunny today,
   A bunny today, a bunny today,
   Oh, hop up and down like a bunny today,
   And turn yourself around!

4. **Variation:** When children know this song well, you may ask them if they would like to add more animal movements—instead of hopping like a bunny, maybe they could stomp like an elephant or waddle like a duck!

Ducky Town

This silly activity includes a lot of different movements for children to explore. They also get to travel to Ducky Town, Froggie Town, Horsey Town, and Birdie Town.

1. The children should be standing in a circle. You may choose whether they should move in place, or if you have space, move around the room. Waddle like a duck, and sing to the tune of "The Acorn Song":

   I'm a duck from Ducky Town,
   I like to waddle all around,
   I waddle up,
   I waddle down, (bend down low while waddling)
   And then I waddle back to Ducky Town! (rise and waddle again)

2. Additional verses:

   I'm a frog from Froggie Town,
   I like to jump all around...
   I'm a horse from Horsey Town,
   I like to gallop all around...
   I'm a bird from Birdie Town,
   I like to fly all around...

3. Ask the children to suggest more animals and "towns."

LEARNING BENEFITS
- Cognitive development (reinforcing the concepts of *up* and *down*)
- Curiosity
- Gross-motor skills (waddling, jumping, galloping)
- Imagination (pretending to be animals)
- Improvisation and creative thinking
- Social skills (sharing ideas and respecting those of others)

Ding-Dong

Who is at the door? That is the funny surprise in this movement activity.

LEARNING BENEFITS

- Curiosity
- Fine-motor skills ("ringing" doorbell, beckoning)
- Gross-motor skills (wiggling, "flying," galloping)
- Imagination (pretending to be animals)
- Improvisation and creative thinking
- Social skills (sharing ideas and respecting those of others)

1. Children should be standing in a circle. Ask them to act out the animal that comes to the door. Sing to the tune of "Twinkle, Twinkle, Little Star" (but a little faster):

   Ding-dong! (press an imaginary doorbell)
   Who's there?
   It's a wiggly worm!
   Wiggling on the doorstep,
   It's a wiggly worm!
   Hi there, hi there, (wave hello)
   Come on in! (beckon with arm)
   It's so nice to meet you, (pretend to shake hands)
   Won't you be my friend? (continue "shaking hands")
   Ding-dong, who's there?
   It's a wiggly worm,
   Wiggling on my doorstep,
   It's a wiggly worm!

2. Additional verses:

   ...a flying bird...flying on my doorstep
   ...a galloping horse...galloping on my doorstep
   ...a jumping frog...jumping on my doorstep

3. Ask the children for their ideas for more animals to ring the doorbell!

4. **Variation:** It does not have to be an animal at the door! It could be a child in your class. Ask if someone would like to be at the door and do a movement. When you choose someone, ask her what her movement will be, so the group will be prepared. Then, you can sing, "Ding-dong, who's there? It's Zamaya! Hopping on one foot, it's Zamaya," and so on.

Activities Using Scarves

Young children love the softness, lightness, and swishiness of scarves. Scarves inspire all kinds of new dance and movement ideas. I like to use 16" x 16" juggling scarves—they produce a very satisfying swish in the air.

Water Dance

I have found this activity to be a good introduction to dancing with scarves. It is very simple and enjoyable for toddlers through kindergartners.

LEARNING BENEFITS

- Auditory discernment (moving differently according to musical cues)
- Fine-motor skills (holding on to scarves)
- Gross-motor skills (using arms and shoulders to move scarves)
- Musical awareness (understanding of slow and fast tempos)
- Spatial skills (respecting the space of the children around them)

1. The children should be standing in a circle. As you pass out the scarves, remind the children to hold them and not let them fall. (Some children will be tempted to drop or throw the scarves.)

2. Tell them that the music they will hear starts out very slowly. Ask them to show you how they could move their scarves slowly. Then explain that, after a while, the music will change to a slightly faster, bouncier beat. Ask them to show you bouncy ways to move the scarves. Remind them to listen to the music and move the way the music tells them to.

3. Play a recording of "Water Dance" by Raffi (available for purchase via online music sites) or any piece of music that has changes in tempo or mood. Children usually respond very well to the magic of the colorful, swishing scarves and enjoy the changes in the tempo.

La-Di-Da-Di-Da

When I was swishing a scarf around one day, I felt like singing, "la-di-da-di-da," and the children I was with thought that was fun and copied me. So I created this activity.

1. The children should be standing in a circle, each holding a scarf in one hand. Moving according to the words of the song, sing to the tune of "Here We Go 'Round the Mulberry Bush":

   Shake it up and shake it down,
   Shake it up and shake it down,
   Shake it up and shake it down,
   And la-di-da-di-da. (swish scarf right and left in sideways figure eight)
   Shake it here and shake it there, (shake scarf to left and right)
   Shake it here and shake it there,
   Shake it here and shake it there,
   And la-di-da-di-da. (swish scarf right and left in sideways figure eight)

2. Additional verses:

   Shake it in front and shake it in back... (shake scarf in front of your body and behind your back)
   Hide your face... and peekaboo!... (cover your face with scarf, then suddenly pull it down to reveal your face)

3. Ask the children to find other ways to move the scarves.

4. **Variation:** Ask the children to come up with other funny words to say on the last line, such as "shooby-dooby-doo" or "bibbly-bibbly-bee." (Try these, and ask the children to think of different ones.)

LEARNING BENEFITS

- Curiosity
- Directionality (up and down, left and right, front and back)
- Gross-motor skills (using arms to move the scarf)
- Improvisation and creative thinking
- Patterns (the first three lines of each verse have the same words; the fourth is different—an AAAB pattern)
- Science (exploring the texture and movement of the scarf)
- Social skills (sharing ideas and respecting those of others)

My Scarf Can Be A...

Scarves lend themselves to lots of pretend play. This activity encourages children to use their imaginations.

LEARNING BENEFITS

- Curiosity
- Fine-motor skills
- Imagination (pretending the scarves are different objects)
- Improvisation and creative thinking
- Science (exploring the texture and movement of the scarves)
- Social skills (sharing ideas and respecting those of others)

1. Place your scarf over your head, holding it together at your chin to reveal your face. Bounce to the beat of the song, and sing to the tune of "Polly Wolly Doodle":

   My scarf can be a hat today,
   My scarf can be a hat,
   My scarf can be a hat today,
   My scarf can be a hat!

2. Place it behind your shoulders, holding it together under your chin, and sing:

   My scarf can be a cape today,
   My scarf can be a cape,
   My scarf can be a cape today,
   My scarf can be a cape!

3. Additional verses:

   My scarf can be a belt today...
   My scarf can be a blanket today... (cuddle it around your shoulders, and lean your head to the side)

4. Ask the children what they would like their scarves to be!

Scarf Color Game

Games about colors are always fun, but sometimes children get overexcited and want to tell everyone what color they have, loudly and repeatedly! Be sure to take a minute before you play this game to say, "Look at your scarf. Think about what color it is, but don't say it out loud. Just listen for when I sing about your color, and then do what the song says." As an alternative, you could take a moment and ask, "Who has a blue scarf?" "Who has an orange scarf?" and so on, before you begin the activity.

1. Distribute the scarves in a variety of colors. The children should be standing in a circle, each holding a scarf. Sing to the tune of the "Dinah, won't you blow?" section of "I've Been Working on the Railroad":

   If you're holding a scarf that's red,
   You can wear it on your head!
   On your head, on your head,
   If your scarf is red.

   If you're holding a scarf that's blue,
   You can shake it on your shoe!
   On your shoe, on your shoe,
   If your scarf is blue.

2. Additional verses:

   ...green...You can jump like a jumping bean!
   ...yellow...You can wave like you're saying, "Hello!"
   ...pink....You can shake it and blink, blink, blink!
   ...brown...Shake it up and shake it down!
   ...if your scarf is purple today,
   *   Swish your scarf and start to sway!*
   ...white...You can fly it like a kite!
   ...if your scarf is orange so bright...
   *   Shake your scarf with all your might!*

LEARNING BENEFITS

- Cognitive skills (colors)
- Curiosity
- Gross-motor skills (reaching, jumping, waving)
- Listening skills (waiting to hear a certain color)

Magic Hat

Everyone would like to have a magic hat, right? Young children certainly would, especially when it allows them to imagine and pretend.

LEARNING BENEFITS

- Curiosity
- Fine-motor skills
- Imagination (pretending to be animals)
- Improvisation and creative thinking
- Kinesthetic awareness (feeling scarf on head)
- Social skills (sharing ideas and respecting those of others)

1. Decide ahead of time whether you will allow the children to move around the room when they are pretending. If you would prefer that they stay seated, then make that clear. Many of the children will move around unless you ask them not to.

2. Have the children put their "magic hats" (scarves) on their heads. Ask them not to take the hats off until the end of the song, when you say, "Now take off the hat!" Put a scarf on your own head, and play the game with them so they understand the idea of pretending to be what the song says. Sing to the tune of "Here We Go Looby Loo":

   When you take off your hat,
   When you take off your hat,
   When you take off your hat,
   You will turn into a cat!
   (spoken) *Now take off the hat!*
   (Say "meow" and curve your "paws" like a cat.)

3. You may also turn into a bird, a tiger, a dog, a pig, and any animal your students request!

4. **Variation:** Ask the children what else the scarf could be. They might decide it should be a magic shoe, a magic cape, or another item of clothing.

Free-Improvisation Ideas for Scarves

When you need more improvisation ideas to stir up children's imaginations, here are some you can try:

- Wear the scarf like a skirt, held at the sides of your waist, and bounce to the beat.
- Shake the scarf really fast, then really slowly.
- Shake the scarf high above your head.
- Squat down, and wiggle the scarf on the floor.
- Ball the scarf up in your hands, and then swish it out.
- Turn around, and watch your scarf swish.
- Move the scarf around by holding one corner, then the next corner, then the next, and so on.
- Roll up the scarf and hold it by both ends, then bounce it to the beat.
- Hold two corners at the top, and lift left and right corners, alternating.
- Hold two corners at the top, and shake the scarf.

LEARNING BENEFITS

- Curiosity
- Fine-motor skills
- Gross-motor skills (reaching, squatting, turning)
- Improvisation and creative thinking
- Science (exploring texture and movement of scarves)

Here are some of my favorite pieces (many versions are available via online music-purchasing sites) to move along to in free-improvisation sessions with scarves:

- "Waltz of the Flowers," *The Nutcracker* by Pyotr Ilyich Tchaikovsky
- "Waltz of the Snowflakes," *The Nutcracker* by Pyotr Ilyich Tchaikovsky
- "Aquarium," *Carnival of the Animals* by Camille Saint-Saëns

Activities Using Spanish Words

A good way to introduce Spanish words to children is through easy movement songs. You can find some on recordings, but you can also make up games using Spanish words to go with familiar tunes. In New Jersey, where I teach, second-language learning is mandated for kindergarten through eighth grade, plus one year in high school, and most preschools begin some introductory language learning. No matter where you live, it is beneficial socially and cognitively for young children to learn words from other languages.

Corre/Camina

This activity provides an easy and fun way to introduce two Spanish words to young children. You can use a variety of tunes to go along with this game.

LEARNING BENEFITS

- Cognitive development and musical awareness (fast and slow movement)
- Curiosity
- Learning Spanish words
- Listening skills (responding to verbal cues)
- Social skills (leading classmates and following peers' directions)

1. *Corre* is pronounced "cor-ay" and means "run." *Camina* is pronounced "cah-mee-nah" and means "walk." Explain these words and their meanings to the children.

2. Tell them that in this game they will run in place when you say, "*Corre!*" and walk in place when you say, "*Camina!*" The challenge is for them not to shout when running (young children tend to do this), so that they can hear when you say, "*Camina!*" when they need to walk.

3. Start by saying, "*Corre!*" (I usually hum a fast tune after this.) After a while, say, "*Camina!*" (I hum in a more leisurely fashion then.)

4. After playing the game a few times, you may choose children to take turns being the leader and saying, "*Corre!*" and "*Camina!*"

Manos

Manos is pronounced "mah-noce" and means "hands." In this activity we not only learn a new Spanish word, but we also think of different ways to keep the beat with our hands.

1. The children may be sitting or standing in a circle. Explain the Spanish word, and sing to the tune of "Old MacDonald":

   Manos, manos, *clap, clap, clap,* (on "*Manos, manos*" hold up your two hands facing out, then clap)
   Clap, clap, clap, clap, clap!
   Manos, manos, *clap, clap, clap,*
   Clap, clap, clap, clap, clap!

2. Additional verses:

   ...shake, shake, shake...
   ...wave, wave, wave...
   ...wiggle, wiggle, wiggle...
   ...catch a star... (reach up with alternating right and left hands to "catch stars")
   ...pat, pat, pat... (pat thighs)

3. Invite the children to think of other ways to keep the beat with their *manos.*

LEARNING BENEFITS

- Curiosity
- Fine-motor skills (clapping, shaking, waving)
- Improvisation and creative thinking
- Learning a word in Spanish
- Social skills (sharing ideas and respecting those of others)

En la Mañana

Mañana is pronounced "mah-nyah-nah" and means "morning." *En la mañana* means "in the morning," so in this activity we act out things that happen in the morning.

LEARNING BENEFITS

- Curiosity
- Gross- and fine-motor skills (stretching, yawning, "eating")
- Improvisation and creative thinking
- Learning Spanish words
- Social skills (sharing ideas and respecting those of others)

1. The children should be standing in a circle. Explain the Spanish words to the children, and sing to the tune of "The Bear Went over the Mountain":
   En la mañana *the sun comes up,* (make the sun rise with your arms like in "The Itsy Bitsy Spider")
   En la mañana *the sun comes up,*
   En la mañana *the sun comes up,*
   That's when the sun comes up. (clap on last line)

2. Additional verses:
   ...I yawn and stretch... (stretch arms as if waking)
   ...I eat my breakfast... (pretend to eat)

3. Ask the children what else they do in the morning: get dressed? brush their teeth? put on their shoes? How will we act out these things?

Dedos Can Wiggle Up

Dedos is pronounced "day-doce" and means "fingers." In this activity we use our fingers to create different movements.

1. Before starting, explain the meaning and pronunciation of *dedos*. Then, sing to the tune of "Here We Go Looby Loo," wiggling your fingers as indicated:

   Dedos *can wiggle up,*

   Dedos *can wiggle down,*

   Dedos *can wiggle up,*

   And 'round and 'round and 'round. (flutter fingers in a circle)

2. Additional verses:

   ...climb up... (make climbing motions)

   ...slide up... (hands held horizontally facing out, slide up and down)

   ...wiggle up fast... (wiggle fingers and sing very fast)

3. Have children think of other motions for their *dedos*.

LEARNING BENEFITS

- Cognitive development (concepts of *up, down,* and *around*)
- Curiosity
- Fine-motor skills
- Improvisation and creative thinking
- Learning a Spanish word
- Social skills (sharing ideas and respecting those of others)

The Rain, the Rain, la Lluvia

Young children have fun with this silly movement song. Encourage them to wiggle their fingers on their heads very gently, to feel like raindrops.

LEARNING BENEFITS

- Curiosity
- Fine-motor skills
- Improvisation and creative thinking
- Kinesthetic awareness (feeling fingers "rain" on head, shoulders, elbows)
- Learning Spanish words
- Social skills (sharing ideas and respecting those of others)

1. The children should be standing in a circle. Explain that *lluvia* is pronounced "you-vee-a" and means "rain." Make a "raining" movement with your fingers wiggling downward on your head while singing to the tune of "My Hat, It Has Three Corners":
   The rain, the rain, la lluvia,
   Is falling on my head,
   The rain, the rain, la lluvia,
   Is falling on my head!

2. Additional verses:
   ...is falling on my shoulders...
   ...is falling on my elbows...
   ...is falling on my shoes...

3. Ask the children for their ideas about where *la lluvia* might fall.

Activities Using American Sign Language

American Sign Language (ASL) is the third most commonly used non-English language in the United States, behind Spanish and Chinese. Marilyn Daniels, a professor of speech communication at Penn State University, states that learning ASL signs "may translate to better... reading ability, larger English vocabularies, and may further both receptive and expressive language development" (2003). It also adds a fun and engaging movement component to songs, stories, and games.

For more help in learning the signs in these activities, visit the American Sign Language Browser at http://commtechlab.msu.edu/sites/aslweb/ browser.htm. It presents short videos of people doing signs for thousands of words.

Potatoes

The ASL sign for *potato* is made by making a fist with the nondominant hand, making a bent *V* sign with the dominant hand to represent a fork, and tapping the back of the fist with the "fork."

LEARNING BENEFITS

- Curiosity
- Fine-motor skills
- Gross-motor skills (reaching to "pull out potatoes")
- Imagination (pretending they are pulling, stirring, eating)
- Learning an ASL word

1. In this activity, we act out how potatoes grow and how we eat them. You might want to discuss with your class the different ways people cook potatoes. Some young children are not aware that french fries are made from potatoes. (They sometimes deny it vehemently when they find out!)

2. The children should be standing in a circle. Sing to the tune of "Sing a Song of Sixpence":

   We like to eat potatoes, (make sign for *potato* and bounce it to the beat)

   They grow under the ground, (point down to ground)

   They grow and grow and grow and grow, (make *potato* sign go up and up)

   They grow without a sound. (make *ssh* sign with finger over lips)

   We pull the potatoes out, and (pretend to pull potatoes out of the ground)

   We cook them in a pot, (pretend to stir)

   We eat and eat and eat and eat, (pretend to eat)

   We like potatoes a lot! (make *potato* sign bounce to the beat again)

   Even children who don't care for potatoes enjoy this activity!

Please Clap Your Hands

The ASL sign for _please_ is made by using your open hand to rub in a circle over your heart. The sign for _thank you_ is made by moving your hand out and down, starting near your mouth as though beginning to blow a kiss. After learning this song, you and the students may use these signs in conversation for extra practice.

1. The children may be sitting or standing. Sing to the tune of "Frère Jacques":

   Please clap your hands, (make the sign for _please_, then clap)
   Please clap your hands,
   Clap, clap, clap,
   Clap, clap, clap,
   Thank you all for clapping, (make sign for _thank you_, then clap)
   Thank you all for clapping,
   Clap, clap, clap.
   Clap, clap, clap.

2. Additional verses:

   Please pat your knees...
   Please pat your shoulders...
   Please nod your head...

3. Have the children suggest additional movements.

LEARNING BENEFITS

- Curiosity
- Fine-motor skills
- Improvisation and creative thinking
- Learning ASL words
- Patterns (each verse has a _please_ section and a _thank you_ section—an AB pattern)
- Social skills (sharing ideas and respecting those of others)

In the Fall

This activity uses the ASL sign for *fall (autumn)* and explores the fun things young children like about fall. The sign for *fall* is made by using your nondominant hand to be a tired tree tilted up near your face. The dominant hand represents the leaves falling, shaking up and down from a diagonal position crossing your chest to a horizontal position near your waist.

1. Children should be standing in a circle. Sing to the tune of "Here We Go 'Round the Mulberry Bush":

   In the fall I jump in the leaves, (make the sign for *fall*, then jump)
   Jump in the leaves, jump in the leaves.
   In the fall I jump in the leaves,
   I jump in the leaves in the fall.

2. Additional verses:

   ...I run around... (run in place)
   ...I bounce a ball... (pretend to bounce a ball)
   ... feel the wind... (make hands swish back and forth like the wind blowing)

3. Ask the children what else they like to do in the fall, and then act their ideas out in the song.

LEARNING BENEFITS

- Curiosity
- Gross-motor skills (jumping, bouncing, swishing hands)
- Improvisation and creative thinking
- Learning an ASL word
- Social skills (sharing ideas and respecting those of others)

Thinking of a Name

The ASL sign for *thinking* is made by using your pointer finger to make a circle by the side of your forehead. This is a quiet, relaxing activity that also helps children learn each other's names.

1. The children should be sitting in a circle. Make the sign for *thinking* when that word is used in the song. Sing to the tune of "Shoo, Fly, Don't Bother Me":

   I'm thinking of a name that starts with a B, (do the
       sign for thinking, then clap to the beat)
   Thinking of a name that starts with a B,
   Thinking of a name that starts with a B,
   The name I'm thinking of is Brendan!

2. Repeat for all the names in the class, if possible. You may want to pause before you announce the name and see if the children can guess it.

LEARNING BENEFITS
- Curiosity
- Fine-motor skills
- Learning an ASL word
- Phonemic awareness (recognizing letters and connecting them to sounds)

Again

The ASL sign for *again* is very easy, even for toddlers—you simply curve your dominant hand and touch all the fingertips to the opposite palm.

LEARNING BENEFITS

- Curiosity
- Fine-motor skills
- Gross-motor skills (bending)
- Kinesthetic awareness (feeling the body moving faster and faster)
- Learning an ASL word

1. This is one of those "faster and faster" songs that always gets children laughing. Sing to the tune of "London Bridge Is Falling Down":

   Head and clap and knees and clap, (touch your head, clap, touch your knees, and clap)
   Knees and clap, knees and clap,
   Head and clap and knees and clap,
   And then we do it again! (on *again*, make the sign for *again*)

2. Repeat a few times, getting a bit faster each time.

Activities Using Inner Listening Skills

Audiation, or inner listening, is the process of hearing music mentally when the sound is not physically present. It is a skill we use every day. How many times, for instance, have you sung "The Alphabet Song" in your head when you are alphabetizing words? You don't really sing out loud, but you hear the song in your mind. When young children use inner listening skills, it increases their auditory memory and musical understanding. It also helps children develop their singing ability, since they are practicing the music whenever they listen to it mentally.

The Rabbit and the Chicken and the Skunk and the Mouse

Children love this very silly song, but it is a bit tricky—I recommend it for four- and five-year-olds. It involves audiation, or the ability to "hear" music in your head. It also requires auditory memory to remember the movements and the self-control to remain silent at certain times in the activity.

1. The children should be sitting in a circle. Tell the children that you are going to teach them a very silly song that has hand movements that go with it. First, demonstrate it for the class. Sing to the tune of "Head and Shoulders, Knees and Toes":

   The rabbit and the chicken and the skunk and the mouse, (make bouncing bunny ears with a *V* sign for the rabbit, flap your "wings" for the chicken, hold your nose for the skunk, and skitter your fingers with hands close together like a mouse's paws for the mouse)

   The rabbit and the chicken and the skunk and the mouse,

   I wish they'd all move out of my house, (hold hands together in a wishing pose on your chest, then point backwards with your thumb)

   The rabbit and the chicken and the skunk and the mouse!

2. Have the children try the song with you, slowly. (You might want to practice it twice.)

3. Verse 2: Sing the song, leaving out the word *rabbit* but making the bunny ears motion.

4. Verse 3: Sing the song, leaving out the words *rabbit* and *chicken* but making the motions.

5. Verse 4: Sing the song, leaving out the words *rabbit*, *chicken*, and *skunk* but making the motions.

6. Verse 5: Sing the song, leaving out the words *rabbit*, *chicken*, *skunk*, and *mouse* but making the motions.

7. Verse 6: Try "singing" the whole song silently, using just the hand motions.

LEARNING BENEFITS
- Audiation (inner listening)
- Auditory memory (remembering verbal cues)
- Curiosity
- Fine-motor skills

About to Sneeze

Like "The Rabbit and the Chicken and the Skunk and the Mouse," this activity challenges students' audiation skills—they will need to "hear" the song in their heads to be able to act out the motions correctly. So again, this is appropriate for four- and five-year-olds, who are beginning to develop this ability.

One surefire way to engage young children is to do an activity with a sneeze in it! There is just something about sneezing that always gets them laughing—and listening.

I also like this activity because I use an unusual movement, wiggling the knees, which is challenging but still well within the skill range of most four- and five-year-olds. They like trying it and are proud of themselves when they can do it.

1. The children should be standing in a circle. Sing to the tune of "The Battle Hymn of the Republic" (it is also the tune to "Little Peter Rabbit"):
   I tap my head (tap head gently with both hands)
   And tap my toes (reach down and tap your toes)
   And wiggle my knees, (wiggle your knees around)
   I tap my head
   And tap my toes
   And wiggle my knees,
   I tap my head
   And tap my toes
   And wiggle my knees,
   Whenever I'm about to sneeze! A-CHOO! (on *whenever I'm about to*, march with just your arms; on *sneeze*, touch your nose; then make a loud "achoo!" sound)
2. Verse 2: Sing the song, leaving out the words *tap my head* but doing the motion.

3. Verse 3: Sing the song, leaving out the words *tap my head* and *tap my toes* but doing the motions.

4. Verse 4: Sing the song, leaving out the words *tap my head*, *tap my toes*, and *wiggle my knees* but doing the motions.

5. Verse 5: "Sing" the entire song silently—even the "A-CHOO!"

LEARNING BENEFITS

- Audiation skills
- Auditory memory (remembering verbal cues)
- Curiosity
- Fine-motor skills (tapping the head, touching the nose)
- Gross-motor skills (tapping toes, wiggling knees)

Fee Fi

This is another good activity for practicing audiation (the ability to "hear" music in your head). Since the tune is familiar, the students can more easily learn and remember the words and the motions that go with them. And it is a lot of fun!

Some children may not be familiar with the word *banjo*. Tell them it is like a guitar, only the body is round and it has steel strings. Better yet, bring in a picture or an actual banjo, if available.

LEARNING BENEFITS

- Audiation (inner listening)
- Auditory memory (remembering verbal cues)
- Curiosity
- Fine-motor skills
- Imagination (pretending to strum a banjo)

1. The children should be sitting in a circle. Sing to the tune of the "Fee fi, fiddly-eye-o" section of "I've Been Working on the Railroad":

   Fee, fi, (hold left hand out to side, palm up, then right hand out to side, palm up)

   Fiddly-eye-o, (point to eye, then form an *O* with thumbs and cupped hands)

   Fee, fi, fiddly-eye-o-o-o-o,

   Fee, fi, fiddly-eye-o.

   Strumming on the old banjo. (pretend you are strumming on a banjo)

2. Verse 2: Sing the song, but leave out the words *fee fi,* and just do the hand motions.

3. Verse 3: Sing the song, but leave out the words *fee fi* and *fiddly-eye,* and just do the hand motions.

4. Verse 4: Sing the song, but leave out the words *fee fi, fiddly-eye,* and *O,* and just do the hand motions.

5. Verse 5: Try to "sing" the song silently, using just the hand motions.

Other Movement Activities

Most of these activities are interactive. Instead of each child performing a movement individually, in these activities they will interact with the other children in the group. This benefits young children by encouraging them to cooperate with others and respond to social cues. For example, a child may need to adjust his pace of movement to match the pace of the group. Interpersonal and social cooperation are difficult developmental tasks for many children, and these activities provide a way to practice in a fun, stress-free environment.

Other activities in this section use different kinds of motion (for instance, walking along a tightrope or creating movements with only their hands) than the activities in previous sections.

Rowing with the Sharks

I have always felt that many traditional early-childhood activities are girl centered. That is one reason I redesigned this song to make it more boy friendly. I have found that both boys and girls have a great time while they also coordinate their movements and use careful listening to cooperate in this activity.

LEARNING BENEFITS

- Curiosity
- Cognitive development (*fast* and *slow*)
- Gross-motor skills (rowing motions)
- Imagination (pretending to be tired, see a shark)
- Improvisation and creative thinking
- Listening skills (rowing fast or slowly depending on verbal cues)
- Social skills (rowing together as a group)

1. The children should be sitting on the floor in a circle, holding hands. Explain that, first, we will just be rowing a boat together. "Row" with hands together while singing:

   Row, row, row your boat, gently down the stream,
   Merrily, merrily, merrily, merrily, life is but a dream.

2. Then ask the children to pretend that they have been rowing all day and they are very tired. How would they row then? Probably slowly. Let them decide how slowly they would row. They might even doze off a bit.

3. Then, uh-oh! Pretend to see a shark. "Let's row away from it as fast as we can!" (You'll be amazed at how quickly children can row away from a shark!)

4. Let the children use their imaginations to see other things in the sea. Are they beautiful, scary, or funny? How would they move in relation to the different objects?

Little Miss Muffet

This game is based on the classic nursery rhyme. Young children love it (I suspect it is because of the scary-but-exciting spider), but it does require some discussion beforehand.

1. Sing the song to the traditional tune (you can also chant it, if you wish), while clapping your hands to the beat:

   Little Miss Muffet sat on her tuffet,
   Eating her curds and whey.
   Along came a spider, who sat down beside her,
   And frightened Miss Muffet away!

2. Ask the children what they think a *tuffet* might be. Someone will usually guess "something to sit on." That is a good guess—tell them it is a low seat or stool. What about *curds and whey?* Well, curds and whey are actually the lumps and liquid found in cottage cheese. Many younger children are not familiar with cottage cheese—with toddlers and two-year-olds, you may just tell them it is a kind of cheese. So here we are learning vocabulary, even if it is rather archaic!

3. Sing the song again, acting it out, pretending you are Little Miss Muffet eating her cheese. Bring out a spider puppet to sit down beside you. Of course, act very frightened at the end!

4. Take turns acting out the rhyme, with Little Miss Muffet (or Little Mister Muffet, if it is a boy) sitting in the middle of the circle, pretending to eat. Make the spider puppet sit next to her, and Little Miss Muffet can look scared and hurry back to her seat.

5. **Variation:** In older groups, some children like to pretend to be the spider themselves to scare Miss Muffet. In fact, you may find that the role of the spider is more popular than the role of Little Miss (or Mister) Muffet!

LEARNING BENEFITS

- Cognitive development (learning the concept of *beside*)
- Curiosity
- Gross-motor skills (crawling like a spider, hurrying back to seat)
- Imagination (pretending to be frightened, pretending to be a spider)
- Social skills (acting out the rhyme with another child)
- Vocabulary (*tuffet, curds and whey*)

Vegetable Soup

This song is one of my students' favorites. I like to play it in the fall when the children are starting to eat soup and other warm foods.

This is a very physical activity, so remind the children ahead of time to be careful of the people around them as they play.

1. Explain that you will be asking, in the song, who wants to be a carrot. Tell the children that if they want to be a carrot, they should raise their hands quietly, and you will choose one of them. Clap to the beat and sing to the tune of "Shoo, Fly, Don't Bother Me":

   Who wants to be a carrot?
   Who wants to be a carrot?
   Who wants to be a carrot?
   Madison wants to be a carrot! (choose a child)

2. Then the "carrot" goes to the middle of the circle and turns around while the rest of the children pretend they're stirring the "soup" and sing to the "I feel, I feel, I feel like a morning star" part:

   I'm stirring, I'm stirring,
   I'm stirring my vegetable soup,
   I'm stirring, I'm stirring,
   I'm stirring my vegetable soup!

3. Continue with other children joining the carrot in the middle:

   Who wants to be a potato?
   ...an onion?
   ...a pea?
   ...some broccoli?
   ...a tomato?
   You can add other vegetables if you wish.

4. I always end by saying that I like a lot of noodles in my soup and ask in the song, "Who wants to be a noodle? ...Everybody wants to be a noodle!" So the whole class is spinning around, and I pretend to stir while singing the "stirring" section.

5. **Variation:** For more fun, when the activity is over you can "taste" the "soup" with an imaginary spoon, decide it needs more salt, sprinkle a pretend salt-shaker over the children, and taste it again. Now it tastes just right. You will have a soup full of giggly vegetables!

LEARNING BENEFITS

- Curiosity
- Fine-motor skills (stirring motion)
- Gross-motor skills (turning around)
- Imagination (pretending to be vegetables)
- Social skills (moving inside the circle with others while respecting their space)
- Vocabulary (*carrot, potato, onion*)

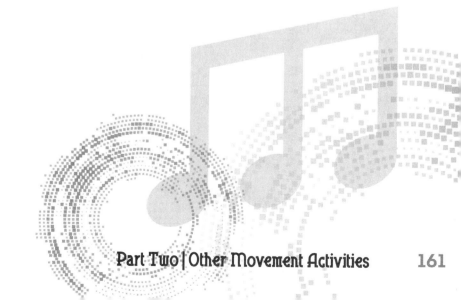

Tightrope with Bells

Children love to do tricks, and I like to include tricky movements in my activities. I try to use movements that are difficult enough to be interesting but not so hard that children get frustrated trying to do them. This activity seems to be a good not-too-hard challenge for young children.

LEARNING BENEFITS

- Balance and coordination (balancing bells on head while walking)
- Curiosity
- Imagination (pretending to be a tightrope walker at the circus)
- Locomotor skills (walking along a line)
- Social skills (taking turns, encouraging classmates)

1. Use the piece "Entry of the Gladiators" by Julius Fucik (available via online music-purchasing sites) to accompany this activity. You (and the children) will recognize this music right away as "the circus song." It adds fun and excitement to the activity.

2. Place a long piece of masking tape along the carpet to be the "tightrope." Let the children take turns being a "tightrope walker" with a twist—they need to balance a bell bracelet on their head while they walk, being careful to stay on the line.

Can You Balance on One Foot?

Balancing on one foot is definitely tricky, but balance is an important developmental skill. This activity helps young children to practice it in an enjoyable, age-appropriate way. Some four- and five-year-olds will be able to master this; some will have fun trying; and some may be too developmentally immature to try it without getting frustrated. Use your judgment and your knowledge of your group's skill levels before you try this activity. When they can get through the song successfully, though, it is a big boost to their self-esteem.

1. The children should be standing in a circle. Demonstrate standing on one foot, and let them try it, then tell them they are going to try to stand on one foot through a whole song.

2. Have the children stand on one foot, and sing to the tune of "Do Your Ears Hang Low?":
   Can you balance on one foot?
   It's not hard if you stay put.
   Can you balance for a while, with a happy little smile?
      (smile brightly and wave head left and right)
   Just don't wiggle, and don't jiggle,
   And be careful not to giggle,
   Can you balance on one foot?

3. It usually makes the children feel more comfortable if you stumble and land on two feet at some point. (You may not have to pretend!) Say, "Oops!" and try standing on one foot again. It emphasizes the fun of trying something, even if you are not perfect the first time.

4. Ask the children if they heard which words in the song rhyme. (They are *wiggle, jiggle,* and *giggle*. Also, *foot* and *put* rhyme.)

5. Remind the children that those who can't quite balance for long will be able to in a while, and that it is good manners to encourage others and not point out their mistakes.

LEARNING BENEFITS
- Balance
- Gross-motor coordination
- Persistence
- Phonemic awareness (rhymes on *wiggle, jiggle,* and *giggle*)
- Social skills (trying something hard together, while supporting and encouraging each other)

The Crunchy Munchy Salad

You will not find too many children's songs about healthy foods. I always hope this activity will inspire interest in eating salad. At least it inspires interest in pretending to be salad!

1. In this activity, you will match the colors children are wearing to various salad vegetables. First tell the children that this game is about salad. The space in the middle of the circle is the salad bowl, and they are going to be the vegetables in the salad. Ask the children to look at their clothes and think about what colors they are wearing. Then tell them that you are going to sing a song about a color. If they are wearing that color, they can be the vegetable you mention and come to the "salad bowl."

2. Sing slowly and clearly to the tune of "A-Hunting We Will Go":
   Oh, if you are wearing red,
   If you are wearing red,
   You can be a tomato,
   And jump in the salad bowl!

3. When all the "tomatoes" are in the salad bowl, ask them to jump while you and the other children clap to the beat and sing to the same tune:
   Oh, the crunchy munchy salad,
   The crunchy munchy salad,
   It's fun to crunch, it's fun to munch,
   The crunchy munchy salad!

4. Continue with other vegetables:
   Green...lettuce
   White...onion
   Orange...carrot
   Brown...potato (or *mushroom*)

5. You may need some fruit, too.

   Blue...blueberry

   Pink...watermelon

   Purple...grape

6. Last but not least...

   Yellow...cheese

7. By now, everyone should be in the salad bowl. Have them stay there while you pretend to pour salad dressing on them. (They love this part.)

8. To maintain order after the game, you may want to ask the tomatoes to return to their seats, then the lettuce, and so on.

LEARNING BENEFITS

- Auditory memory (remembering musical cues to jump and clap)
- Cognitive development (colors)
- Curiosity
- Fine-motor skills (clapping)
- Gross-motor skills (jumping)
- Imagination (pretending to be vegetables)
- Listening skills (waiting for their colors to be called)
- Vocabulary (*lettuce, onion, tomato, carrot*)

It's Snowing, It's Snowing

This is a fun activity for a snowy day or after reading a story about snow. It is funny, but the gentle movement makes it relaxing and good for winding down.

LEARNING BENEFITS

- Curiosity
- Fine-motor skills ("snowing" with fingers)
- Kinesthetic awareness (feeling "snowflakes" on their heads)
- Social skills (taking turns)

1. Ask the children if they know where snow comes from. Some will say "the sky," but some will usually know that it falls from clouds. Then ask them if anyone would like to be a snow cloud.

2. Choose a child to be the "snow cloud," and tell the other children to close their eyes. The "snow cloud" walks around the middle of the circle while you all sing to the tune of "It's Raining, It's Pouring":
   It's snowing, it's snowing,
   The cold wind is blowing,
   Can you feel the snowflakes
   Falling on your head?

3. Then the "snow cloud" gets to surprise a classmate by gently "snowing" on her head with soft fingertips. The "snow cloud" sits again and the snowed-on child gets to be the next "snow cloud."

4. **Variation:** The "snowed-on" child could become a new snow cloud, while the old one remains. Now you have two snow clouds and twice the snow! Continue until all the children are snow clouds, and they can all take turns snowing on you before they return to their seats.

Hand Dancing

I was inspired to create this activity while watching some beautiful Asian Indian dancing featuring intricate, delicate hand gestures. I have since learned that these gestures, called *hasta mudras*, have very specific meanings in Indian classical dance. This kind of dance is an art form that requires years of practice to master.

I found it fascinating that these dancers could make so many different, unique movements and shapes with their hands. As I suspected, young children can use the idea of dancing using only their hands to come up with amazing, inventive ideas.

1. For this activity, use Indian music as background. Two pieces I like are "Eastern Journey" by the Biddu Orchestra (available on iTunes), which has a very rhythmic, Bollywood-type flavor, and "Blind Man's Journey" (available on http://play.kindermusik.com/en/tracks/4126-sorida).

2. Tell the children that they are going to do a special dance using only their hands. At first, they should copy your movements; at some point, hand them the reins and let individual children suggest hand movements. You might want to go around the circle and have each child contribute a hand movement.

3. Here are some hand-movement ideas to get you started (repeat each movement several times):
   - Hands held vertically, palms facing out, bounce hands in place
   - Hands held vertically, palms facing out, bounce left and right hands alternately
   - Hands held horizontally, palms down, move hands out to sides of body and back in
   - Hands held horizontally, palms down, move both hands up and down
   - Hands held horizontally, palms down, move both hands to the front and then back toward your body

■ Hands held vertically, palms facing out, bend left hand down to horizontal position, then change so right hand is horizontal and left hand is vertical

■ Hands held horizontally, palms down, "walk" your hands to the beat

■ Hands held together in prayer position, bounce up and down

■ Hands held together in prayer position, lean hands to left and right

■ Hands held horizontally, wiggle fingers

■ Hands held vertically, palms out, fingers splayed, lean hands to left and right

■ Hands held vertically, palms out, fingers splayed, flex fingers as if grabbing something and flex back

■ Hands held horizontally, palms down, fingers splayed, flutter like eyelashes

■ Make fists open and close

4. **Variation:** Just for fun, you can have the children stretch out their legs in front of them and do "foot dancing," trying out different ways to move their feet to the beat.

Stomp to My Lou

This very simple activity can be used early in the school year as a confidence builder to accustom children to thinking of their own ideas for movement. The well-known tune makes it easy for them to focus on the movements, without having to learn an unfamiliar song at the same time.

1. The children should be standing in a circle. Stomp your foot to the beat while singing to the tune of "Skip to My Lou":

   Stomp, stomp, stomp to my Lou,
   Stomp, stomp, stomp to my Lou,
   Stomp, stomp, stomp to my Lou,
   Stomp to my Lou, my darlin'.

2. Additional verses:

   Wave, wave, wave to my Lou... (wave hand to the beat)

   Twist, twist, twist to my Lou... (with hands on waist, twist upper torso side to side)

   Nod, nod, nod to my Lou... (nod head to the beat)

3. Ask the children to contribute their ideas—what else could we do "to my Lou"?

LEARNING BENEFITS

- Curiosity
- Gross-motor skills (stomping, waving, twisting)
- Improvisation and creative thinking
- Patterns (the first three lines of each verse have the same words; the fourth line is different—an AAAB pattern)
- Social skills (sharing ideas and respecting those of others)

I Can Touch the Sky

Children move, bend, and stretch their bodies in many directions in this movement activity. It is perfect as a stretching and warm-up activity for a music-and-movement session.

LEARNING BENEFITS

- Curiosity
- Gross-motor skills (stretching, diving, bending, reaching)
- Improvisation and creative thinking
- Social skills (sharing ideas and respecting those of others)

1. The children should be standing in a circle. Ask them to pretend it is nighttime and reach up and try to touch the sky. If you see some children simply raising their hands up, encourage everyone to "really stretch as high as you can." Sing to the tune of "The Farmer in the Dell":

   Oh, I can touch the sky,

   Touch all the stars I see, (wiggle fingers around to "touch" different stars)

   I'll catch a star (reach up and "grab" with one hand)

   With both my hands, (reach up with other hand so you're holding the "star" with both hands)

   And hold it close to me. (bring hand down to hold "star" close to your heart)

2. Additional verses:

   I'll dive into the ocean, (pretend to dive way down)

   Touch all the fish I see,

   I'll catch a fish with both my hands,

   And hold it close to me.

   (At the end of this verse, have the children throw their fishes back into the ocean.)

3. Ask, "What if it's daytime? Let's catch a cloud."

   Oh, I can touch the sky,

   Touch all the clouds I see...

4. Say, "Now let's go to the beach and touch the sand."

   Oh, I can touch the sand,

   Touch all the shells I see...

5. Ask the children for more ideas. If they are stuck, offer hints. If you touch an apple tree, what could you catch? If you bent down and touched the ground outside, what could you catch?

Run, Run, Run

No need to worry—I am not suggesting that you let young children run around the room! We run in place for this easy improvisatory activity.

1. The children should be standing in a circle. Run in place and sing to the tune of "Hurry, Hurry, Drive the Fire Truck":

   Run, run, run, and tap your shoulders, (on *tap*, stop running and tap your shoulders to the beat)
   Run, run, run, and tap your shoulders,
   Run, run, run, and tap your shoulders,
   Run, run, run, run, run!

2. Additional verses:

   Run, run, run, and pat your tummy...
   Run, run, run, and tickle your elbows...
   Run, run, run, and wiggle your fingers...

3. Then invite the children to think of other movements we can do after we "run, run, run."

4. **Variation:** Instead of "Run, Run, Run," this activity could just as easily be "Jump, Jump, Jump," "March, March, March," or other movements your students suggest.

LEARNING BENEFITS

- Curiosity
- Fine-motor skills (tapping shoulders, patting tummy)
- Gross-motor skills (running in place)
- Improvisation and creative thinking
- Kinesthetic awareness (feeling fingers on shoulders, hands on tummy, fingers on elbows, and so on)
- Patterns (movement pattern is running, tapping, running, tapping, running, tapping, running—an ABABABA pattern)
- Social skills (sharing ideas and respecting those of others)

Beanie Animal Minuet

Early childhood educators know that many times a young child will talk more readily and openly to a puppet than to a real person. Similarly, making a puppet or stuffed animal dance often brings out more free and creative movement than when a child dances with her own body. There is sometimes less self-consciousness and more of a willingness to be silly and a little wild. In fact, I once taught a class of two-and-a-half-year-olds in which most of the children kept stuffed animals with them all through music class. They would make the animals wave hello to me and clap in time to the music, as well as dance. It clearly made them feel comfortable and brought a lot of fun to music time.

In my experience, the easiest animals to use are the small beanie-type animals. I collected these from my own (older) children and from flea markets and yard sales until I had a good supply. I found that beanie animals love to dance to all kinds of music! I find them especially useful to introduce music that may be unfamiliar to young children, such as music from other cultures, jazz, and classical music.

1. This minuet from the "String Quartet in E Major, Op. 11, No. 5" by Luigi Boccherini (if you type in "Boccherini Minuet" on a music-purchasing site you will find it) is charming and fun for children to make beanie animals dance to. It is also in 3/4 time, meaning there are three beats to a measure. You will want to emphasize the 1-2-3, 1-2-3 pattern in your dancing. You might want to use this piece for a special dance on a "Teddy Bear Day" when children bring in their teddy bears.

2. The children should be sitting in a circle, each holding a beanie animal. Tell the children that you have brought in some special beautiful music

for the animals to dance to. Of course, the children may make their animals dance any way they want to, but here are some suggestions to get you started (repeat each movement several times):

- Have animals bow to the animals on their right and left
- Have animals bounce or jump in place to the beat
- Have animals take three steps out and three steps in
- Have animals take three steps to the left and back
- Have animals take three steps to the right and back
- Make animals turn around
- Make animals twirl in the air
- Make animals bounce on your shoulder
- Make animals dance on their (the animals') heads
- Make animals bounce in place while leaning left and right, alternately
- Make animals "fly"
- Make animals clap their hands
- Make animals kick their feet

LEARNING BENEFITS
- Curiosity
- Fine-motor skills
- Imagination (pretending toy animals can dance)
- Improvisation and creative thinking
- Musical awareness (responding to classical music)
- Social skills (sharing ideas and respecting those of others)

Can You Clap, Clap, Clap?

The old song "Do Your Ears Hang Low?" supplies the tune for this activity. Be sure to start pretty slowly, because there are a lot of motions for the children to learn and keep up with. Young children enjoy how this song gets faster and faster. Remind them that getting mixed up trying to keep the pace of the movement is half the fun. This should just be silly and enjoyable, not stressful.

LEARNING BENEFITS

- Cognitive development and musical awareness (slow and fast music and movement)
- Curiosity
- Fine-motor skills (clapping, "eating," holding "phone")
- Gross-motor skills (flapping arms, knocking, stamping)

1. The children should be sitting in a circle with their legs stretched out in front of them, knees bent. Sing to the tune of "Do Your Ears Hang Low?":

   Can you clap, clap, clap? (do three claps on "clap, clap, clap," emphasizing the rhythm)

   Can you flappy-flappy-flap? (tuck hands under your armpits and "flap" like a chicken)

   Can you knock upon the door? (pretend to knock on a door in front of you)

   Stamp your feet upon the floor? (stamp feet)

   Can you eat your macaroni? (pretend to eat)

   While you're talking on the phone-y, (pretend to talk on phone)

   Can you clap, clap, clap?

2. Repeat the song a few times, getting progressively faster and faster.

St. Patrick's Day Hopscotch

Most young children are not really aware of what St. Patrick's Day is about. I asked a four-year-old once why we celebrate St. Patrick's Day, and he said, "To wear green socks." When we talk about celebrating the country of Ireland, they usually understand. But, I have found that listening to authentic Irish music in the context of a game is more engaging and meaningful.

1. Make four or five large (about 10 inches in diameter) cardboard circles with green shamrocks drawn on them. Explain that shamrocks are a kind of clover that is a symbol of Ireland. Tape the shamrocks to the floor with masking tape, in a row, about 6 inches apart.

2. Have the children take turns jumping on each shamrock. Play some authentic Irish music in the background to accompany this activity. One of my favorite Irish pieces is "Mulvihill's/Irish Washerwoman/Whelan's" by Sean Tyrell (available via music-purchasing websites). Tyrell plays many Irish string instruments beautifully, and the music is invigorating.

3. Some children may jump sedately; some may do big, flashy jumps. Some may try hopping on one foot. But remember, if the children miss the shamrocks or even just choose to walk on them rather than jump, that is okay. This is not a test—it is just for fun.

4. **Variation:** You can do hopscotch-style games for any occasion. Make cardboard cutouts of hearts for Valentine's Day, flags for the Fourth of July, pumpkins for Halloween, and so on, choosing appropriate music for the children to hop along with.

LEARNING BENEFITS
- Coordination (jumping along a line of shamrock shapes)
- Curiosity
- Locomotor skills (jumping, hopping, or walking)
- Multicultural awareness (responding in movement to Irish music)
- Social skills (taking turns)

Because It's Halloween

I enjoy Halloween, and of course it is an exciting time for young children. But, I feel that too many Halloween songs, stories, and activities overplay the scary and ghoulish side of the holiday. This activity focuses on the fun, playful aspects of Halloween.

LEARNING BENEFITS

- Curiosity
- Gross-motor skills ("flying," prowling, crawling)
- Imagination (pretending to be bats, cats, spiders)
- Improvisation and creative thinking
- Movement vocabulary (*prowling, crawling, wobbling*)
- Social skills (sharing ideas and respecting those of others)

1. The children should be standing in a circle. Decide if you want the children to move around through the room or stay in their position in the circle. Sing to the tune of "The Bear Went over the Mountain":
   The bats are flying around, (fly like a bat)
   The bats are flying around,
   The bats are flying around,
   Because it's Halloween!

2. Additional verses:
   The black cats are prowling around... (prowl with arms, hands making paws)
   The spiders are crawling around... (crawl in place or around the room)
   The pumpkins are wobbling around... (have arms make semicircles at sides and wobble on your feet)
   The children are walking around... (walk in place or around the room)

3. Ask the children to contribute other Halloween-related ideas for movement. They may want to do movements based on their costumes, such as "The princesses are dancing around."

Swimming in the Ocean

This chant is appropriate for summer months or whenever you are reading a story or doing a unit on the ocean.

1. The children should be standing in a circle. Do swimming motions with your arms while you rhythmically chant:

   Swimming in the ocean,
   Swimming in the sea,
   Swimming in the ocean,
   With a one-two-three! (jump in place three times)

2. Additional verses:

   Splashing in the ocean... (pretend to splash hands in the water)
   Fishy in the ocean... (make fishy face and "swim" with hands together like a fish)
   Seaweed in the ocean... (wiggle fingers like seaweed)
   Sharks in the ocean... (put hands together on top of head to make a "fin")

3. Ask the children for more animals and other things that you might see in the ocean, and act their ideas out in the song.

LEARNING BENEFITS
- Curiosity
- Gross-motor skills (swimming motions, jumping, splashing)
- Imagination (pretending to be swimming and splashing, pretending to be animals)
- Improvisation and creative thinking
- Rhythmic awareness (strong rhythmic chanting)
- Social skills (sharing ideas and respecting those of others)

Bendio

Few things seem funnier to young children than making up nonsense words. Actually, the words in this song are kind of half-nonsense, since they are based on real words. They sound funny enough to amuse children—and inspire them to create funny words of their own.

LEARNING BENEFITS

- Curiosity
- Gross-motor skills (bending, "swimming," shrugging)
- Improvisation and creative thinking
- Phonemic awareness (making nonsense words by adding the *io* sound to each movement word)
- Socials skills (sharing ideas and respecting those of others)

1. The children should be standing in a circle. Put your hands on your waist, and bend your knees to the beat while you sing to the tune of "The Acorn Song":
   Bendy, bendy, bendio,
   Bendy, bendy, bendio,
   Bendy, bendy, bendio,
   Bendy, bendy, bendio!

2. Then make swimming motions with your arms and sing:
   Swimmy, swimmy, swimmio,
   Swimmy, swimmy, swimmio,
   Swimmy, swimmy, swimmio,
   Swimmy, swimmy, swimmio!

3. Additional verses:
   Shruggy, shruggy, shruggio... (shrug shoulders to the beat)
   Jumpy, jumpy, jumpio... (jump to the beat)

4. Let the children think up their own movements that can be made into silly words according to the pattern of the song.

References

Baney, Cynthia Ensign. 1999. "Wired for Sound: The Essential Connection between Music and Development." *Early Childhood News* March/April.

Bonawitz, Elizabeth, Patrick Shafto, Hyowon Gweon, Noah D. Goodman, Elizabeth Spelke, and Laura Schulz. 2011. "The Double-Edged Sword of Pedagogy: Instruction Limits Spontaneous Exploration and Discovery." *Cognition* 120(3): 322–330.

Buchsbaum, Daphna, Alison Gopnik, Thomas Griffiths, and Patrick Shafto. 2011. "Children's Imitation of Causal Action Sequences Is Influenced by Statistical and Pedagogical Evidence." *Cognition* 120(2): 331–340.

Copeland, Kristen A., Susan N. Sherman, Cassandra A. Kendeigh, Heidi J. Kalkwarf, and Brian E. Saelens. 2012. "Societal Values and Policies May Curtail Preschool Children's Physical Activity in Child Care Centers." *Pediatrics* 129(2): 265–274.

Daniels, Marilyn. 2003. "Using a Signed Language as a Second Language for Kindergarten Students." *Child Study Journal* 33(1): 53–70.

FitDay. 2013. "Dance classes: How Moving to the Beat Can Help You Enjoy Exercise." http://www.fitday.com/fitness-articles/fitness/exercises/dance-classes-how-moving-to-the-beat-can-help-you-enjoy-exercise.html

Geist, Kamile, Eugene Geist, and Kathleen Kuznik. 2012. "The Patterns of Music: Young Children Learning Mathematics through Beat, Rhythm and Melody." *Young Children* 67(1): 74–79.

Keck, Kristi. 2009. "Obama Wants to Overhaul Education from 'Cradle to Career.'" CNNPolitics.com. http://www.cnn.com/2009/POLITICS/03/10/obama.education.

Miranda, Carolina A. n.d. "Why Creative Education Is Important for Kids." *Parenting.* www.parenting.com/article/creative-play

National Association for Music Education. 2013. "The School Music Program: A New Vision: The K–12 National Standards, PreK Standards, and What They Mean to Music Educators." NAfME. Reston, VA: NAfME. http://musiced.nafme.org/resources/the-school-music-program-a-new-vision

Neelly, Linda. 2001. "Developmentally Appropriate Music Practice: Children Learn What They Live." *Young Children* 56(3): 32–37.

Oesterreich, Lesia. 1995. "Ages & Stages—Five-Year-Olds." In *Iowa Family Child Care Handbook*. Ames, IA: Iowa State University Extension.

Perry, Bruce. 2001. "Curiosity: The Fuel of Development." *Early Childhood Today* (March).

Pica, Rae. 2010. "Linking Literacy and Movement." *Young Children* 65(6): 72–73.

Shahidullah, Sara, and Peter Hepper. 1992. "Hearing in the Fetus: Prenatal Detection of Deafness." *International Journal of Prenatal and Perinatal Studies* 4(3): 235–240.

Sloutsky, Vladimir, and Christopher Robinson. 2008. "The Role of Words and Sounds in Infants' Visual Processing: From Overshadowing to Attentional Tuning." *Cognitive Science* 32(2): 342–365.

Stinson, Sue. 1988. *Dance for Young Children: Finding the Magic in Movement*. Reston, VA: The American Alliance for Health, Physical Education, Recreation, and Dance.

Uvnas Moberg, Kerstin. 2003. *The Oxytocin Factor: Tapping the Hormone of Calm, Love, and Healing*. Cambridge, MA: Da Capo.

Von Stumm, Sophie, Benedikt Hell, and Tomas Chamorro-Premuzic. 2011. "The Hungry Mind: Intellectual Curiosity Is the Third Pillar of Academic Performance." *Perspectives on Psychological Science* 6(6): 574–588.

Zentner, Marcel, and Tuomas Eerola. 2010. "Rhythmic Engagement with Music in Infancy." *Proceedings of the National Academy of Sciences* 107(13): 5768–5773.

Index